Emerging Trends in Real Estate®
2016

Contents

Editorial Leadership Team

Emerging Trends Chairs

Mitchell M. Roschelle, PwC
Kathleen B. Carey, Urban Land Institute

Principal Advisers and Contributing Authors

Andrew Warren, PwC
Anita Kramer, Urban Land Institute

Author

Hugh F. Kelly

Senior Advisers

Christopher J. Potter, PwC, Canada
Miriam Gurza, PwC, Canada

Contributors

Sarene Marshall, Urban Land Institute
Stockton Williams, Urban Land Institute

ULI Editorial and Production Staff

James A. Mulligan, Senior Editor
David James Rose, Managing Editor/Manuscript Editor
Betsy Van Buskirk, Creative Director
Anne Morgan, Cover Design
Deanna Pineda, Muse Advertising Design, Designer
Craig Chapman, Senior Director of Publishing Operations
Marc Andrew Curtin, Project Assistant
Rebecca Lassman, Project Intern

PwC Advisers and Contributing Researchers

Adam Boutros*
Aki Dellaportas
Alex Tanchez*
Alexander P. Stimpfl
Allen Baker*
Amy Brohman*
Amy E. Olson
Andrew Alperstein
Andrew Paterson*
Andrew Popert*
Andrew Stansfield
Annie Labbé*
Brian J. O'Donnell
Brian T. Nerney
Brion L. Sharpe
Bud Thomas
Carlo Bruno
Charles P. Alford
Chase C. Evans
Chris Potter*
Chris Vangou*
Christina Howton*
Christine Lattanzio
Christopher A. Mill
Christopher L. Nicholaou
Constance Chow*
Courtney S. McNeil
Dan Crowley
Daniel J. O'Neill
Daniel D'Archivio*
David Baldwin
David Baranick
David Khan*
David M. Voss
David Seaman
David Yee*
Deborah Dumoulin*
Dominique Fortier*
Donald Flinn*
Doug Purdie*
Douglas B. Struckman
Dwayne MacKay*
Edward Sheeran
Eli Rabin
Elliot Kung
Emily Pillars
Eric Andrew*
Eric St-Amour*
Ernest Hudson*
Eugene Chan
Frank Magliocco*
Fred Cassano*
Gabrielle Mendiola*
Haley M. Anderson
Heather M. Lashway
Howard Ng*
Howard Quon*
Ian Gunn*
Isabelle Morgan
Jackie Kelly
Jacqueline Kinneary
Jaime D. Phillips
James Oswald
Janaki Sekaran
Janice McDonald*
Janice Zaloudek
Jasen Kwong*
Jeff Kiley
Jill Lising*
John Gottfried
John Paul Pressey*
Joseph H. Schechter
Joseph R. Fierro
Joshua Hookkee

Julia Powell
Kelly Nobis
Kelsey Edelen
Kristen Conner
Kristen D. Naughton
Kristianne M. Marchart
LaRon E. York
Laura Daniels*
Lawrence A. Goodfield
Leah Waldrum
Leandra M. Charsky
Lisa Guerrero
Lona Mathis
Lori-Ann Beausoleil*
Mark Williams
Martin J. Schreiber
Martina Scheuer
Marvin A. Thomas
Mary Wilson-Smith*
Mathilde C. Hauswirth
Matthew Berkowitz
Maxime Lessard*
Meghan O'Brien
Michael Anthony
Michael Shields*
Michael T. Grillo
Mike Herman
Miriam Gurza*
Nadia King*
Nadja Ibrahim*
Naveli Thomas*
Neal P. Kopec
Nicholas Mitchell
Nick Ethier*
Nicole M. Stroud
Noah Weichselbaum
Oliver Reichel
Philippe Thieren*
Rajen Shah*
Rajveer Hundal*
Renee Sarria
Richard Fournier
Rick Barnay*
Rob Christmas*
Rob Sciaudone
Ron Bidulka*
Ron Walsh*
Rosanna Musto*
Ross Sinclair*
Ryan Dumais
Ryan Thomas*
Sean Hiebert*
Seth E. Kemper
Shannon M. Comolli
Shareen Yew
Stephan Gianoplus
Stephen W. Crisafulli
Steve Tyler
Steven Weisenberger
Susan M. Smith
Tim Bodner
Timothy C. Conlon
Tracy L. Howard
Victoria M. Music
Warren Marr
Wendi Pope*
Wendy J. Wendeborn
Wesley Mark*
William Croteau
William Hux
William Keating
Yvens Faustin

* Canada-based.

Notice to Readers

Emerging Trends in Real Estate® is a trends and forecast publication now in its 37th edition, and is one of the most highly regarded and widely read forecast reports in the real estate industry. *Emerging Trends in Real Estate® 2016*, undertaken jointly by PwC and the Urban Land Institute, provides an outlook on real estate investment and development trends, real estate finance and capital markets, property sectors, metropolitan areas, and other real estate issues throughout the United States and Canada.

Emerging Trends in Real Estate® 2016 reflects the views of individuals who completed surveys or were interviewed as a part of the research process for this report. The views expressed herein, including all comments appearing in quotes, are obtained exclusively from these surveys and interviews and do not express the opinions of either PwC or ULI. Interviewees and survey participants represent a wide range of industry experts, including investors, fund managers, developers, property companies, lenders, brokers, advisers, and consultants. ULI and PwC researchers personally interviewed 404 individuals and survey responses were received from 1,465 individuals, whose company affiliations are broken down below.

Private property owner or developer	34.3%
Real estate services firm	26.5%
Institutional/equity investor or investment manager	11.5%
Bank, lender, or securitized lender	7.4%
Real estate brokerage	6.5%
Homebuilder or residential land developer	5.5%
Equity REIT or publicly listed real estate property company	3.1%
Other entity	2.6%
Private REIT or nontraded real estate property company	2.1%
Mortgage REIT or real estate debt investor	0.4%

Throughout the publication, the views of interviewees and/or survey respondents have been presented as direct quotations from the participant without attribution to any particular participant. A list of the interview participants in this year's study who chose to be identified appears at the end of this report, but it should be noted that all interviewees are given the option to remain anonymous regarding their participation. In several cases, quotes contained herein were obtained from interviewees who are not listed. Readers are cautioned not to attempt to attribute any quote to a specific individual or company.

To all who helped, the Urban Land Institute and PwC extend sincere thanks for sharing valuable time and expertise. Without the involvement of these many individuals, this report would not have been possible.

Coordinating Offense and Defense in 2016

"You can never forget about cycles, but the next 24 months look doggone good for real estate."

Every major college and NFL football team sees its game plan shaped by its offensive and defensive coordinators, working in concert with the head coach. The coordinators are expected to have both technical and strategic skills, the ability to work under pressure, and the capacity to adjust to rapidly changing conditions.

For the offense, the coordinator is charged with marshalling the team's resources to maximize opportunities and to translate them into points on the road to victory. For the defense, the coordinator is constantly assessing risks, both before and during the game, and countering them. In limiting the competition's advantages, the defensive coordinator seeks to put his team in the best position on the field by managing adversity and,

Exhibit 1-2 Emerging Trends Barometer 2016

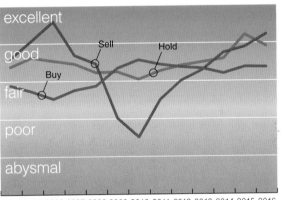

Source: *Emerging Trends in Real Estate 2016* survey.
Note: Based on U.S. respondents only.

as much as possible, turning an opponent's risk taking into an opportunity for his own squad.

For real estate, 2016 will see investors, developers, lenders, users, and service firms relying upon intense and sophisticated coordination of both their offensive and defensive game plans. In an ever more competitive environment, with well-capitalized players crowding the field, disciplined attention to strategy and to execution is critical to success.

A lending officer at a large financial institution said, "You can never forget about cycles, but the next 24 months look doggone good for real estate." At the same time, as one senior capital markets executive said, "The first 15 minutes of any committee discussion is on the potential risk in the deal." We've learned some lessons in the not-too-distant past.

Exhibit 1-1 U.S. Real Estate Returns and Economic Growth

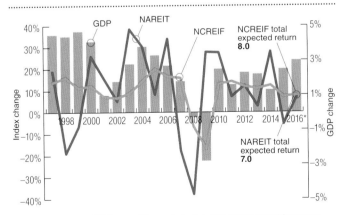

Sources: NCREIF, NAREIT, Bureau of Economic Analysis/U.S. Department of Commerce, *World Economic Outlook*, *Emerging Trends in Real Estate 2016* survey.

* GDP forecasts are from *World Economic Outlook*.

Note: NCREIF/NAREIT data for 2015 are annualized as of first-quarter 2015. Forecasts for 2016 are based on the *Emerging Trends in Real Estate 2016* survey.

Exhibit 1-3 Firm Profitability Prospects for 2016

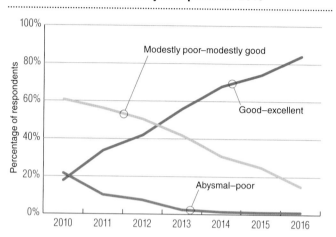

Source: *Emerging Trends in Real Estate* surveys.

Real estate has become ever more dynamic as it adapts to a networked world. Everything is connected to everything else, so market participants cannot afford to ignore developments well beyond the property markets themselves. The major forces of globalization, technology, urbanization, and demography are constantly interacting with each other. A lapse of attention or a misstep in execution can result in being blindsided, foiling even a well-considered plan of action.

Because of this, it is important to understand that none of the trends we identify and discuss should be considered in isolation. The "Keep It Simple, Stupid" rule has its strengths, but only if it also recognizes that a complex world punishes any overly rigid approach to change in the markets. In business, as in biology, adaptation is the key to survival and competitive advantage.

Exhibit 1-4 Real Estate Business Prospects

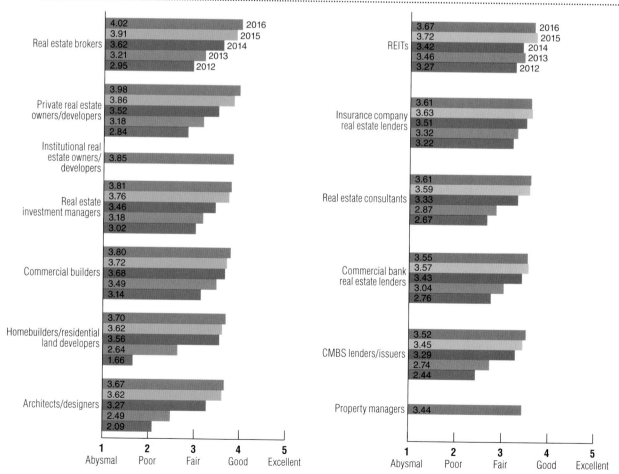

Source: *Emerging Trends in Real Estate* surveys.

Exhibit 1-5 Survey Market Outlook Change, 2010 to 2016

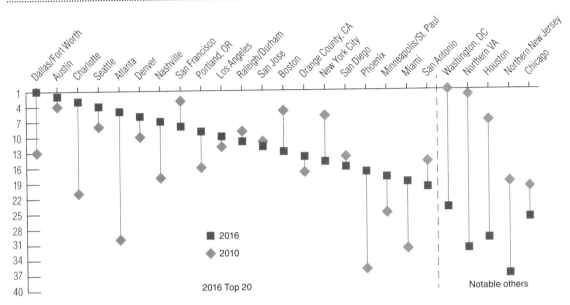

Source: *Emerging Trends in Real Estate* surveys.

So as we discuss the top trends for 2016, we will be emphasizing granularity, the weaving together of several strands of change, and the continuing capacity of the economy and the real estate markets to surprise by their flexibility, resilience, and innovation as both local and macro forces compel ever-greater open-mindedness about the future.

1. 18-Hour Cities 2.0

Last year, *Emerging Trends* identified the rise of the 18-hour city. This year, the real estate industry is expressing growing confidence in the potential investment returns in these markets. We are finding a tangible desire to place a rising share of investment capital in attractive markets outside the 24-hour gateway cities.

Global as well as domestic investors are casting wider nets as they look at U.S. real estate markets. One such investor, at a large international institution, marveled at the number of secondary markets that are suddenly "hip." Austin, Denver, San Diego, and San Antonio are examples, and rightly so. They rank in the top ten markets for entrepreneurship in the 2015 Kauffman Foundation study, and all four are in *Emerging Trends 2016*'s list of top 20 markets for real estate investment and development.

What supports this trend? To start, strengthening U.S. macroeconomic performance is bolstering absorption and improving occupancy in the majority of American real estate markets. Secondly, the 18-hour cities have seen more moderate cap-rate

compression, and so provide an opportunity for superior yields. Investors themselves are demonstrating greater risk tolerance, moving gradually from defense to offense as their playing field position improves. And, lastly, the inexorable expansion of data availability has generated more confidence that decisions about secondary market opportunities can be grounded in good statistical evidence.

The 18-hour cities have been consistently making headway in replicating pieces of what makes the gateway cities so attractive. The development and application of technology make it possible for these markets to offer the benefits of a larger urban area at a significantly lower cost. In addition, a number of the markets in the top 20 rankings of this year's survey are consistently tagged as "cool" markets that are expanding on their own unique culture.

Should the market be concerned that this wider investor interest could diminish in the face of a downturn? Although 18-hour cities and all higher-growth markets have historically been more volatile than their gateway counterparts, there are factors that could diminish the volatility going forward. During the current economic expansion, the capital markets have demonstrated a much greater degree of restraint when it comes to funding new development. So the 18-hour cities face lower-than-average supply pressure, compared with history. Investors, meanwhile, have become more sophisticated. And the greater information across all markets, mentioned above, allows investors to have

Exhibit 1-6 **Change in Value, by Market Category and Property Type, 12 months through June 2015**

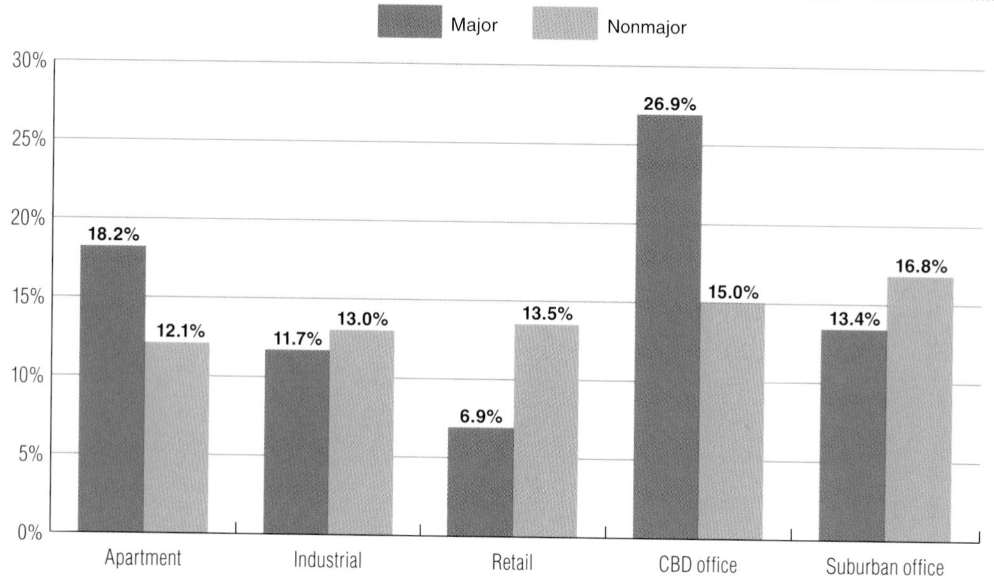

Sources: Moody's and Real Capital Analytics.

a laser focus on their investment, focused on more precisely defined areas and asset characteristics within a submarket or neighborhood. The belief that "anywhere in the market is good" is likely a thing of the past.

An ever-restless search for returns persists, and deals are framed on a risk/reward matrix. As an executive with a private equity investor explained in his interview, "In Nashville, we bought an office building for a 7.25 cap. We plan to redo the lobby, roll the leases to market, hold for four years, and then sell. Nashville is a strong secondary market with some risk, but the price was much more reasonable than core assets in primary markets." That's an 18-hour city story, a deal that works in a vibrant downtown that is drawing residents and businesses to the core.

Going forward, this trend should intensify. More capital is available than a handful of 24-hour markets can absorb.

2. Next Stop: the Suburbs . . . What Is a Suburb?

"The suburbs are a long way from dead," said one interviewee emphatically. Another industry veteran counseled, "There are only about ten dynamic downtowns in the county; the rest of the areas, people are in the suburbs." As prices have risen in the core gateway markets, it is apparent that a fresh look at suburban opportunities is gaining favor.

Many feel that time is on the suburbs' side. They argue that the deferral of marriage and family formation by millennials, and the related preference for downtown living in denser, more active "mating markets," is just that: deferral. Eventually, the logic goes, generation Y will follow the baby boomers' path and head to the suburbs in the child-rearing years. That may very well be, and numbers are on the side of that argument as well. Survey results from ULI earlier in 2015 show that a smaller number of millennials prefer to live in the city than currently do and, conversely, a larger number of millennials prefer to live in the suburbs than currently do. Another ULI survey shows that six out of ten gen-Y respondents expect to live in a detached single-family home five years from now (although these results did not specifically indicate location). It should be pointed out that, overall, there is a slightly larger group of millennials who ultimately prefer city living (37 percent) to suburban living (29 percent), but the gap between the two locations is expected to be smaller than current location patterns (46 percent and 24 percent, respectively). There is enough of this 80 million–plus generation intending to relocate to the suburbs to make an impact.

An economist with a national real estate data firm observed, however, that "this group won't move to the suburbs of their parents. The attractive suburbs will be more like the airline hub-and-spoke model. These 'diet urban' locations will offer urban and suburban benefits." The critical descriptors seem to be suburbs that are close-in, transit-oriented, and mixed-use. A 2015 National Association of Realtors/Portland State University study

Exhibit 1-7 Current and Desired Location—Cities, Suburbs, Rural/Small Towns, by Generation

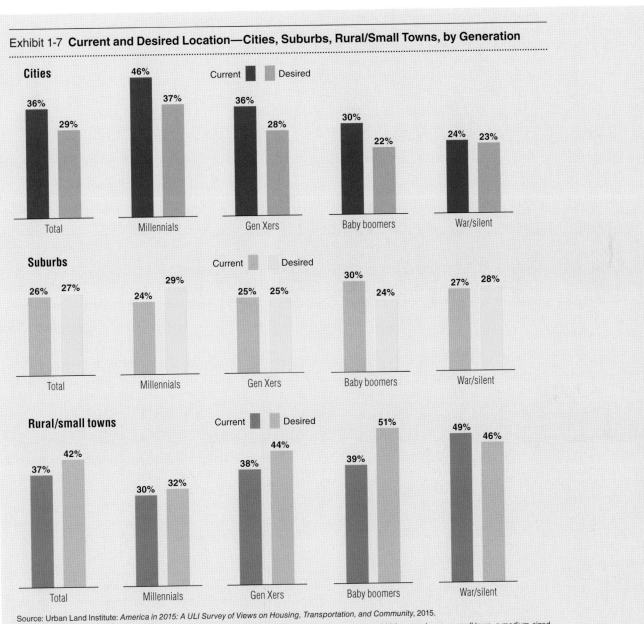

Source: Urban Land Institute: *America in 2015: A ULI Survey of Views on Housing, Transportation, and Community,* 2015.

Note: Response to *America in 2015* survey question: "If you could live anyplace in the next five years, would it be a rural area, a small town, a medium-sized city, a big city, a suburb within a 20-minute drive of a city, a suburb farther than a 20-minute drive to a city, or something else?"

Exhibit 1-8 Current Location of Millennials within Cities

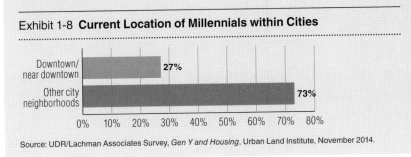

Source: UDR/Lachman Associates Survey, *Gen Y and Housing,* Urban Land Institute, November 2014.

Exhibit 1-9 Detail of Current and Desired City Location—Medium-Sized vs. Big City, by Generation

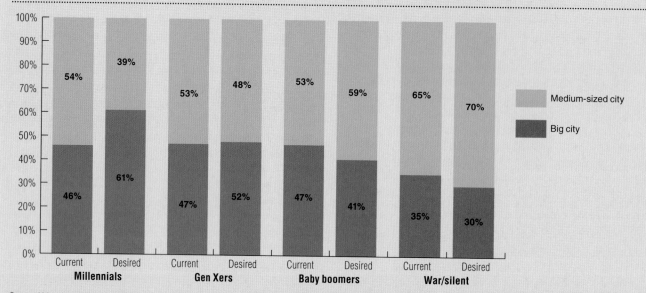

Source: Urban Land Institute: *America in 2015: A ULI Survey of Views on Housing, Transportation, and Community*, 2015.

Note: Drawn from response to *America in 2015* survey question: "If you could live anyplace in the next five years, would it be a rural area, a small town, a medium-sized city, a big city, a suburb within a 20-minute drive of a city, a suburb farther than a 20-minute drive to a city, or something else?"

Exhibit 1-10 Detail of Current and Desired Suburban Location—Suburbs within 20 Minutes vs. Farther Than 20 Minutes from City, by Generation

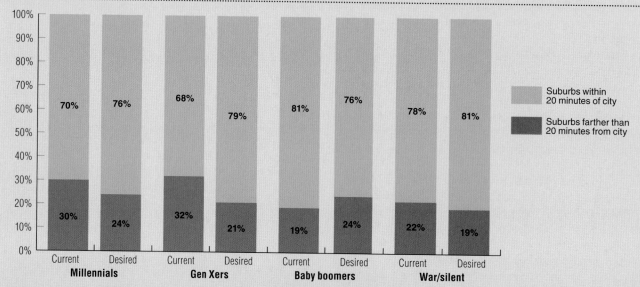

Source: Urban Land Institute: *America in 2015: A ULI Survey of Views on Housing, Transportation, and Community*, 2015.

Note: Drawn from response to *America in 2015* survey question: "If you could live anyplace in the next five years, would it be a rural area, a small town, a medium-sized city, a big city, a suburb within a 20-minute drive of a city, a suburb farther than a 20-minute drive to a city, or something else?"

found that millennials prefer walking over driving by 12 percentage points (see trend 7). One investment manager said that "transportation, not affordability or schools" will be the key driver in a world where two-income households are the social norm.

So, how do these cross currents sort themselves out?

The interaction between jobs and homes is the dynamic that must be carefully understood. Since 2002, job growth (in annual percentage terms) has been higher in the core than the periphery in the majority of top 40 U.S. metropolitan areas. That trend accelerated during the Great Recession and in the immediate post-recession years. This was true for the usual suspects like New York City and San Francisco. But it was also true for Austin, Charlotte, Nashville, and Portland, and for cities like Hartford, Milwaukee, Philadelphia, Pittsburgh, and Oklahoma City as well. And access to these expanding employment opportunities is one of the keys to suburbs with future growth potential.

Still, the suburbs, obviously, are not starting from scratch. Even in the big metro areas, suburbs represent a major share of the existing jobs base. In the top 40 metro areas, 84 percent of all jobs are outside the center-city core. That is the basis for optimism for the suburban future. The configuration (and reconfiguration) of suburban commercial real estate will play a role in building on the existing employment base.

And the configuration of the suburbs is not standing still. More "suburban downtowns" are densifying, especially if they have a 20-minute transportation link to center-city jobs, Main Street shopping, and their own employment generators. These suburbs exhibit many of the attributes of an 18-hour city. These are typically in metro areas where close-in suburbs can both access center-city job growth and act as employment nodes in their own right. And they have the advantage of being less costly than the densest coastal markets. Three out of four millennials preferred such close-in (within 20 minutes of the city) locations if they considered suburban choices.

In Texas, San Antonio joins Dallas and Houston in suburban-dominated job growth. San Diego and Phoenix are in this club as well. Denver's growth marginally favors its suburbs. And even in cities like Chicago, which has been seeing a trend of corporate in-migration from suburb to center, suburban offices have been marking positive absorption and a slow but measurable decline in vacancies. Granularity trumps generalizing in the discussion of the future of suburbs, as it does in other trends discussed in this report.

As in all real estate discussions, location matters and generalizations based on U.S. averages are less relevant. Where the jobs are growing will shape the trend of residential choices over time. It would be a mistake to paint that trend with too broad a brush. But the suburbs may adopt Mark Twain's legendary comment that reports of his death were "greatly exaggerated."

3. Offices: Barometer of Change

On the subject of jobs, the office sector has been benefiting from the strengthening employment numbers in this maturing recovery. Employment is up by more than 2.9 million year-over-year, as it has been since late 2014, and the July growth rate for jobs was a solid 2.1 percent. Job gains have now spread to the vast majority of metro areas, with New York/Northern New Jersey (168,900), Los Angeles (152,000), and Dallas/Fort Worth (117,800) leading in absolute change, and only a few metro areas registering moderate decreases.

With office-using jobs, as tallied by a national brokerage firm, accounting for 39 percent of the employment gain, both central business district (CBD) and suburban office absorption has been brisk, bringing vacancy down 90 basis points and rents up 2.9 percent year-over-year. The outlook for the year ahead is "more of the same."

Redesign of office space to do away with walls and cubicles— and the rethinking of "work" that goes along with it—remain prominent in the minds of our interviewees. It is no longer an issue of overall space per employee compression. Some see the redesign as a way to accommodate an alteration in work style itself; others view it as a workforce capture tool—key to attracting and keeping the desired talent; and for others, it's both. And hip, cool open spaces are not just for startups. Corporate space is accommodating a mix of open areas and a variety of private or semiprivate configurations.

Interestingly, one veteran of the insurance industry remarked, "Insurance companies, decades ago, had these big open offices with desks next to each other. The floor plan was like 100,000 square feet, with big signs that hung from the ceiling that said 'Area 1-J' or 'Area 3.' It was old-school: they had the regular employee dining room and the officers' dining room, but in both cases employees could get lunch for free. I just went to a social media company's building in San Francisco. It reminded me that what's old is new again: open space and a cafeteria where lunch is free."

Entrepreneurial businesses—often seen as the key to a vibrant local economy—urban or suburban, also are contributing to changes in office space, as startups have special space needs.

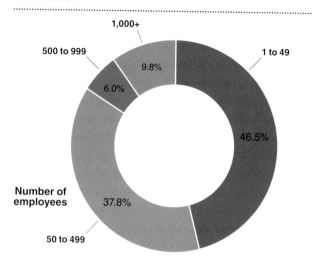

Exhibit 1-11 Share of Job Growth by Company Size, since 2013

- 1,000+
- 500 to 999: 6.0%
- 9.8%
- 1 to 49: 46.5%
- Number of employees
- 50 to 499: 37.8%

Sources: U.S. Bureau of Labor Statistics; Moody's Analytics, as of June 30, 2014.

This is a significant opportunity for the office market, with the U.S. Government Accountability Office estimating "the contingent workforce" (self-employed and unincorporated workers) at 8 percent of the workforce, or 11 million jobs.

Coworking space firms have been actively providing for this emerging element of office workers. Computer coders, business consultants, lawyers, and other knowledge workers are among those taking on space through coworking venues, which have become a major office leasing force in some large markets. This spreads across the geography of the United States.

Entrepreneurs and so-called gig workers are the customer mainstays for such tenants' companies. The business model for coworking companies, incredibly, is based upon levering up the price of conventional office space, even in such expensive markets as Manhattan—which has the highest concentration of coworking firms of any office market. The coworking sponsor leases space from the primary landlord, and then subleases by the desk, the private office, or the suite at a premium, while providing a menu of amenities and the promise of collaboration and synergy, as well as a more professional environment than a wi-fi–enabled coffee shop.

There is, of course, risk in the fixed obligation of the basic lease, but the reported operating margin for coworking firms is reported to be about 30 percent and their growth trajectory has been spectacular. In the New York area, such firms have branched out into Brooklyn and Hoboken, New Jersey. Los

Angeles, Chicago, D.C., San Francisco, Miami, Dallas, and Austin also are target markets for coworking. There are niche players focusing on health care technology, engineering and design, women-owned businesses, and even entrepreneurs focused on social and environmental causes. Depending upon the specialization, amenities range from conference rooms, to car-sharing memberships, to three-dimensional printer access. The range of innovation and experimentation is impressive.

Traditional landlords have embraced the coworking enterprises up to now. Not only do these firms represent immediate market demand for office space, but some see them as the private sector laboratory for "incubator space" that hitherto depended on public or institutional subsidies for the most part.

Emerging Trends interviewees did have some reservations about jumping on the bandwagon, however. Skeptics included a prominent academic and consultant who looked at the sharing membership model and told us, "Do I want to be a tenant in a building where you have 30,000 members who can just drop by and use the space? Forget about this space taken separately; think about the rest of the tenants. . . . I don't know what office building you've been in lately, but you don't 'just stop by' the modern office building post-9/11, security-wise."

Perhaps. But the real estate market seems to be figuring out issues like that. And, meanwhile, coworking spaces are not generating the same kind of regulatory push-back as the apps for ride sharing and room sharing. In the coworking spaces, then, we have entrepreneurial innovation matched up with industry acceptance and at least a benign noninterference from public regulators. Is this a small part of the real estate industry future? Probably. Will it be growing? Most assuredly. One more reason we'll see changes in office space? For sure.

Altogether, the speed at which all these changes appear to be taking place is reflected in interviewees' unusually frequent mention of repositioning and reuse of existing assets.

4. A Housing Option for Everyone

If the "work" component of "live/work/play" is evolving, so is the "live" element—housing. We normally think of change in terms of trends or cycles. Sometimes, we acknowledge patterns of maturation. But the global financial crisis began with disruptive change in the bursting of the housing bubble, which, in turn, has been sorting itself out in a "change of state" whereby homeownership is pulling back from the nearly 70 percent of households seen at the extreme of the bubble to 63.4 percent in the second quarter of 2015.

Exhibit 1-12 **Decline in U.S. Homeownership, 1994 to Present, by Generation**

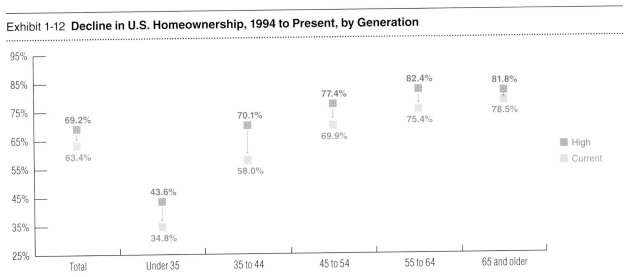

Source: U.S. Census Bureau, Table 19: Homeownership Rates by Age of Householder: 1994 to Present.

As the market sorts itself out, a reasonable expectation is for the homeownership rate to settle in a narrow range around its 50-year average of 65 percent. In the short run, that means the advantage remains with investors and developers in the rental housing sector. Over the longer haul, though, it means that housing demand will be greater across all residential segments.

Economic and demographic factors are influencing the housing market as it deals with issues around providing the type of housing desired by the peak of the baby boom generation, aging millennials, a population making an urban/suburban choice, and finding a way to provide affordable housing to support a vibrant workforce.

Cohousing solutions, micro housing, and other design trends are addressing some of the scarcity and lifestyle issues shaping household preferences. One company, for example, is targeting an age segment as young as the late 40s, who may want community amenities like catered meals, happy hours, shared recreation—and who might become the market for more senior-oriented facilities in later decades of life. We see a trend toward greater diversity in demand and supply across different sectors of the housing market, not to mention the migration of housing styles from one target market to another. An example is the expansion of the student housing model of renting by the bed being applied to a nonstudent market. The concept of renting your own bedroom and bathroom in a group setting may well appeal to millennials even after they have graduated.

Housing is a field where it pays to look "under the equator." By that, we mean that the tendency of analysts (as well as investors and developers) to focus on averages or medians can gravely miss key statistical points that can illuminate both opportunities and risks in the marketplace. The impact of big data on real estate should improve the situation, but only if the data are used to the fullest. Superior profit potential has skewed recent housing production toward the luxury end of product. What is not so obvious is that a shortfall of supply in the mid-to-lower end of the residential market is putting upward pressure on pricing for such units, exacerbating already severe affordability issues.

Affordable and workforce housing is ranked higher in importance in *Emerging Trends* surveys this year than in the last five years, and the "Issues to Watch" section later in this chapter looks at some looming regulatory issues of concern to the industry. The pressures already exist, and are building. Since housing affects everyone, it is no wonder that voters will be pushing politicians for action. Creative ideas, though, will likely depend upon the real estate sector's savvy if they are going to be effective.

Getting ahead of the pressures would be a salutary trend for the industry. Elements of success would mean developing housing products targeted to a variety of income-range cohorts. Some would be rental, some ownership, some rent-to-own. Sharp pencils will be needed to delineate the amounts and the form of government supports. Tax credits, flexible zoning, public/private finance tools, and land trusts are all possible avenues to be explored. Developing improved housing options for everyone, however, is passing from the realm of "nice to do" to "must do." That's going to be shaping the housing trends going forward.

5. Parking for Change

Should we be phasing out parking lots and parking structures even before the widespread adoption of the autonomous vehicle (a.k.a., the driverless car)? Miles traveled by car for those people 34 years old or younger are down 23 percent. The American Automobile Association reports that the percentage of high school seniors with driver's licenses declined from 85 percent to 73 percent between 1996 and 2010, with federal data suggesting that the decline has continued since 2010. The new Yankee Stadium, built in 2008, provided 9,000 parking slots for its 50,000 seating capacity. But that has turned out to be too many, since most fans come by mass transit, and the parking structure is left at just 43 percent occupancy.

Many interlocking trends come into play where parking is concerned. The automobile shaped cities and suburbs, influenced building and zone codes, and helped form the psyche of a couple of generations after the end of World War II. Siting real estate development often involved identifying not only the nearest freeway cloverleaf, but even whether a right or left turn from the access street was needed. Was land so dear that structured parking was a required solution, or could acres be devoted to striped asphalt for shoppers or workers? How many spaces per residential unit? How many per 1,000 square feet of commercial space?

And now, in an era of change, what's next?

Exhibit 1-13 **Automobile Drivers, as a Percentage of All Commuters**

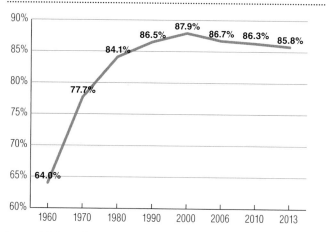

Sources: U.S. Census Bureau, 1960–2000; American Community Survey, 2006–2013.

Exhibit 1-14 **Importance of Issues for Real Estate in 2016**

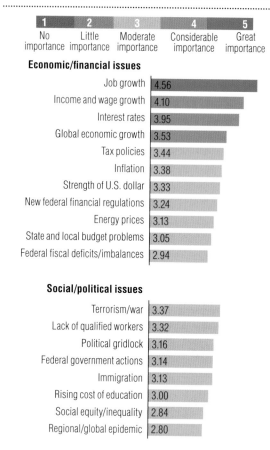

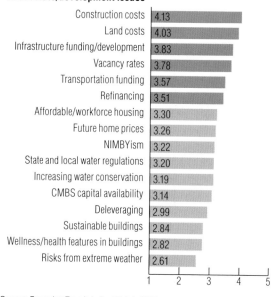

Source: *Emerging Trends in Real Estate 2016* survey.

Climate Change and Real Estate

Are the risks recognized?

This year's *Emerging Trends in Real Estate* survey reveals the real estate industry's lukewarm opinions on how climate change—or government actions to address it—might affect their business. Compared with their thoughts on issues like job growth and construction costs, respondents placed much less importance on the risks of extreme weather, energy prices, sustainable buildings, water conservation, and water regulations (see exhibit 1-14).

Why this difference in rankings?

Regarding extreme weather (which ranked lowest), for example, data from the National Oceanic and Atmospheric Administration reveal that 178 "$1 billion weather disasters"—including droughts, wildfires, hurricanes, floods, and winter storms—occurred from 1980 to 2014. The average event cost $5.8 billion, much of that directly to property, while losses in other sectors (e.g., agriculture and tourism) clearly ripple to affect real estate. The science is clear on the upward trend of disasters like these, given rising global temperatures, changes in rainfall, and warming oceans.

Alarmed by these impacts, the public sector is responding and efforts are underway. California, for instance, has adopted strict water conservation measures in the face of historic drought. With them, golf courses and swimming pools become difficult amenities to maintain, while efficient building features become imperatives. Motivated to address not just climate change effects, but also their cause, more than 30 U.S. jurisdictions have passed energy benchmarking or disclosure laws, echoing the approach of ULI's Greenprint Center for Building Performance. And numerous cities have incorporated LEED-like standards into their green building codes, making them mandatory. These measures and others—like the President's Clean Power Plan—should dramatically increase demand for greener buildings, and may even affect energy prices.

So, why the low rankings? Perhaps these issues are obvious, and are already being considered? (*Emerging Trends* interviewees indicated that many see LEED measures as "second nature," for example.) Or maybe it is simply a matter of mismatched timescales—with climate change impacts perceived as beyond the investment horizon for most real estate projects? Attitudes on that front may shift: This year,

26 percent of *Emerging Trends* respondents report a ten-year or longer time horizon for investing, compared with 16 percent last year. Another hypothesis for these results is the perception that climate change requires collective action at a significant scale.

Cities see things differently.

To compare *Emerging Trends* respondents' perspectives with those of city leaders, we collaborated with CDP—an organization that works to transform the way the world does business to prevent dangerous climate change and protect natural resources. CDP uses measurement, transparency, and accountability to drive positive change in the world of business and investment, and holds the world's largest collection globally of self-reported climate change, water, and forest-risk data from cities and companies.

Risks are recognized.

Forty-six U.S. jurisdictions—from New York City and San Francisco to Aspen, Colorado, and Arlington County, Virginia—publicly disclosed responses to CDP's 2015 information request. CDP's data reveal that many U.S. mayors recognize significant risks from climate change:

- 91 percent said that current and/or anticipated effects of climate change present a significant risk to their city;

- 87 percent said their cities face social risks as a result of climate change [including the loss of traditional jobs];

- 76 percent said that the effects of climate change could threaten the ability of businesses to operate successfully in their city; and

- 74 percent said they foresee substantive risks to their city's water supply in the short or long term.

Of the 245 expected climate change effects disclosed by the cities asked, 58 percent were categorized as current or short-term.

The public sector takes action.

Cities don't just see these challenges; they are acting to address them. Many of these strategies could have impacts on real estate, including the following:

Addressing energy use	Addressing water risks (too much and too little)
Setting citywide green-house gas (GHG) reduction targets	Water use restrictions
Setting citywide renew-able energy and electricity targets	Water conservation incentives
Taking specific actions to reduce GHG emissions from the building sector via: • Building codes and standards • Building performance rating and reporting • Energy efficiency and retrofitting* • On-site renewable energy generation* *Including through codes and incentives	Water metering
	Stormwater management, including fees or ordinances, or green infrastructure incentives
	Use of nonpotable water inside (e.g., via permitting graywater systems)
	Use of nonpotable water outside (e.g., for landscaping)

City Strategies to Reduce Climate Change–Related Risks to Infrastructure, Citizens, and Business	
Atlanta	Creating incentives for water-efficient equipment and appliances to lessen the risk of more intense droughts.
Austin	Setting a 140-gallon-per-capita daily water goal and revising the water conservation code to address long-term drought conditions.
Denver	Developing a recycled-water program that uses treated wastewater for irrigation and other non-potable uses to combat water scarcity.
New York	Published *A Stronger, More Resilient New York*, which led to "the passage of more than a dozen new laws to make new construction in the floodplain more resilient" to increasingly strong storms and associated flooding.
Phoenix	Increasing the tree canopy from 9 percent to 25 percent to counteract the effect of hotter summers.
Seattle	Providing incentives and technical assistance for green roofs to absorb more intense rainfall.

Top markets move to increase resilience.

Municipal leaders are acting for many reasons. One reason for their action is because some of the very strategies that reduce climate-changing carbon emissions and help buffer climate-induced extreme weather also make cities healthier and wealthier, making them more attractive to employers and residents. Or, as someone speaking on behalf of Austin, Texas, noted in response to CDP's 2015 information request: "By reducing greenhouse gas emissions and better managing water resources, we will also have cleaner creeks, less air pollution, and other ancillary benefits."

A number of the cities that ranked in the top 20 in the *Emerging Trends* survey (see chapter 3) were those asked by CDP about their strategies for reducing climate change–related risks. These include the following:

Disclosure about risks (and actions to address threats) provides the real estate industry with important transparency around market conditions; it can help cities and businesses align their efforts to address climate change together; and it helps asset owners in developing strategies for their own portfolios.

Industry is acting, too.

Some in the industry are beginning to incorporate resilience thinking and adaptation measures into their businesses. When *Emerging Trends* respondents were asked what measures, if any, they were taking to address risks posed by extreme weather, several key strategies rose to the top:

• Installing backup and on-site power;

• Investing in higher-quality construction to withstand risks (often above code);

• Avoiding construction in high-risk areas;

• Conducting risk assessments that incorporate severe weather impacts;

• Securing enhanced insurance; and

• Developing emergency management, disaster recovery, and contingency plans.

The urbanization trend and gen-Y preferences already are suggesting that existing parking represents a suboptimal use of land. In both 24-hour cities and 18-hour cities, that is fomenting change. In the highly dense San Francisco market, a pilot program is using variable, demand-responsive fees for both metered and garage parking. In Minneapolis, the traditional one-parking-spot-per-unit rule is giving way to a zero-parking requirement for small (i.e., with fewer than 50 units) apartment developments and a 50 percent reduction in required parking for larger buildings outside downtown, provided they are within a quarter-mile of mass transit running at 15-minute frequencies or greater. Seattle has a new apartment development with a walk score of 98 ("walkers' paradise level") with little parking to start with, but even that little amount is thought to provide excess capacity.

And in Los Angeles, the avatar of the automobile-oriented city, development consultants are thinking about the city's expanding mass transit. "If there is a transit line coming, how do you think about parking in the short run, and can the parking structure be reused for something later? We are looking at a project right now where there will be an extension of one of the train/subway lines, but it could be ten to 15 years away. So you're going to have to build the parking structure, but maybe there is a way to build the parking structure where it can convert to something else in the future." In the inner-ring Washington, D.C., suburb of Bethesda, Maryland, surface parking lots in business parks are already giving way to mixed-use developments with an emphasis on multifamily housing.

Even if we still have a ways to go before we reach the point where we forget that the gas is on the right and the brake is on the left, we will be seeing change trending in the parking patterns of real estate developments. "How cool would it be," that development consultant mused, "if I looked out my window and saw a park instead of a parking lot?"

With lowering the overall cost of construction ranked the number-two issue of importance in the *Emerging Trends in Real Estate 2016* survey, it is easy to see why a Jetsons-like future is capturing the industry's imagination. "Years away" is the consensus of our interviewees, but this is an emerging trend caught in its early stages.

It may seem far-fetched, but the pace of technological change and the consumer's willingness to adopt and adapt suggest that the future may come faster than many expect. For this trend, call the offensive coordinator and figure out the best way to get down the field.

6. Infrastructure: Network It! Brand It!

"The U.S. is losing the battle globally," when it comes to infrastructure, complained one investment manager interviewed this year. "What is our problem?"

The conventional approach to infrastructure improvement is utterly disheartening. The most recent (2013) American Society of Civil Engineers (ASCE) Infrastructure Report Card give the United States a grade of D+. At present, state-by-state updating is going on, and the results are not showing much improvement. Arizona rates a C, as does Georgia. ASCE scores Utah a bit better at C+, but Illinois, Iowa, and Virginia get only a C–. And none of these states is in the oldest region of the nation—the New England/Mid-Atlantic corridor—or the heart of the factory belt in Ohio and Michigan. The ASCE estimate of $3.6 trillion in infrastructure spending needed by 2020 seems way, way out of reach.

Clearly, there is a lot of need to play defense, to prioritize urgent repair and maintenance, and to tackle critical needs in areas like water supply and distribution, aviation, highway bottlenecks and rail safety. With voters in many parts of the country loathe to approve local and state bond issues, public financing is a tough sell. Yet it can be done, as Colorado has demonstrated in passing bond referendums repeatedly, and as the state of Washington is now doing to address its transportation needs.

Many have put hope in public/private partnerships and in vehicles like infrastructure real estate investment trusts (REITs). But the REIT market has focused more on clearly commercial assets, like cellphone towers, energy pipelines, transmission networks, and solar generation than on roads, dams, bridges, and hazardous waste disposal. So public money—where available—needs to go almost exclusively to urgent needs, rather than toward important future needs.

Nevertheless, some creative plans are shifting toward playing offense. High-frequency bus networks, for instance, provide greater transit capacity with superior flexibility and lower cost than fixed-rail operations—especially in less dense cities. Bus rapid transit is often effectively connected to other transit modes such as rail stations or park-and-ride hubs. Minneapolis, Portland (Oregon), Omaha, and Austin have installed high-frequency systems, and Columbus (Ohio), Houston, and Los Angeles have plans in the works.

The private sector has stepped up as well, as one private equity manager noted, "The tech firms are providing bus service, paying some of the costs of freeway exits, even investing in educational facilities." That's not purely charity. The idea is helping to better conditions that attract and retain productive employees.

With traffic congestion costing U.S. businesses and individuals $124 billion per year and with interest in shorter commutes and general walkability growing, here is where infrastructure improvement meets the 18-hour city and the densifying suburb. Places that address this intersection well will trend upward. Places that don't will be competitively disadvantaged. And with a denser network of transit, soaring land costs around transit nodes can be mitigated, with multiplier effects on reducing housing and commercial property development costs as well.

Green infrastructure, another creative instance, is a growing field with aspects of both offense and defense. On offense, an expanding set of tools is available for water management for both local governments and private developers. Permeable pavement, green rooftops, greener parking lots, rainwater harvesting, and other strategies are being employed in New York, Philadelphia, Chicago, Milwaukee, and Seattle, among other large and midsized cities. With the recent evidence of increased storm severity and frequency, these are not only quality-of-life tactics; they also have the defensive strength of dealing preemptively with potentially massive repair and replacement needs. Many localities support private efforts with either rebates or tax advantages, as in Portland, Oregon's Grey to Green initiative. State and local governments, commendably, have stepped up while Congress has dawdled.

As the need to do more with little (let's not concede "less") becomes more acute, a greater attention to innovative solutions to America's massive infrastructure needs is likely to mark the latter half of this decade and beyond.

7. Food Is Getting Bigger and Closer

This may be the ultimate in niche property types: adaptive use with a vengeance (or at least with veggies).

The classic theory of urban places relegates agriculture to the hinterlands, as virtually every kind of vertical construction has superior "highest-and-best-use" characteristics, bringing greater investment returns to land value than growing food. This is absolutely true in most cases. But there are places in more cities than we might imagine where neighborhood land is cheap or older buildings sit idle, and where median incomes are low and the need for fresh food is high. Some are the "hollowed out" areas of Detroit as well as Camden and Newark, New Jersey. But there is a surprisingly significant level of activity in places like Brooklyn, Chicago, Philadelphia, and Washington, D.C., where "foodies" of all generations abound.

"Small potatoes," some might think. While it is true that fruits, vegetables, and products like honey grown in urban environments are no threat to large-scale agribusiness, there is surprising scale to a number of operations. New York City is home to one operation that produces more than 300 tons of vegetables in three hydroponic operations in Brooklyn and Queens. In Chicago, a local business has grown its output to about a million pounds of salad greens and herbs, and contracts with four dozen upscale supermarkets. Detroit's community and commercial farming operations brought 400,000 pounds of food to market in 2014. The term *locavore* has entered the vocabulary of the cuisine cognoscenti.

This, not incidentally, fits hand in glove with the phenomenon of specialty restaurants buoying shopping centers, generating traffic, holding customers for longer periods, and creating "buzz." Foodies are at the sweet spot of retailers' desired demographics—upscale, knowledgeable, and spending-oriented.

In the Ironbound neighborhood of Newark, a 69,000-square-foot former steel factory is being converted into the world's largest indoor vertical farm. The $30 million investment has attracted institutional capital as well as public dollars from the city of Newark and the state of New Jersey. The Ironbound is poised to be for Newark what revitalizing neighborhoods have been just across the harbor in Brooklyn.

What is the "trend" here? Are we likely to see barns and silos dotting our cityscapes? No, that is hardly the point. What is important—and trending—is the new vision that has urban land as that most precious and flexible of resources. The idea that the end of one productive use of a real estate asset spells the extinction of value and the sunsetting of opportunity is an idea whose time is over. Just as the reinvention of the suburbs is an emergent story for the decade ahead, so is the creative adaptation of inner-city uses.

Vegetables aren't the only things sprouting. So is productive activity in places that have long lain fallow.

8. Consolidation Breeds Specialization

If "size matters," that is not the same as "bigger is better." The playing field itself is changing. While size and scale have brought advantage over the years, the evolutionary trends in development, equity investment, and lending are showing that "small can be powerful" as well.

This works on many levels. Developers find it hard to access the best capital unless they have scale; but this means fitting the quality demands of conservative lenders. That requires niche

Exhibit 1-15 Time Horizon for Investing

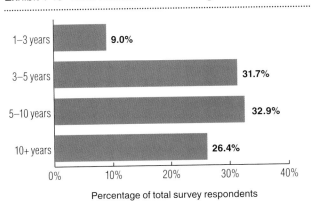

- 1–3 years: **9.0%**
- 3–5 years: **31.7%**
- 5–10 years: **32.9%**
- 10+ years: **26.4%**

Percentage of total survey respondents

Source: *Emerging Trends in Real Estate* surveys.

Note: Based on U.S. respondents only.

lenders can fund the smaller projects, and small developers with their lenders may be accessing the most innovative parts of the business. Also: think brokerage and fund management.

Firms may find themselves in the middle and will need to choose which side—smaller or larger—they wish to be on. A Chicago developer who had long operated as an independent with the capacity to execute high-end urban construction recently moved under the umbrella of a large firm with cross-border businesses. He said, "The builders and owners of property now are entirely different. Small builders just aren't designed to withstand cycles." He also cited "the pursuit costs" of deals— not only having substantial equity that will stay at risk, but also the length of time that capital is at risk. "With the average pursuit of a significant deal taking a minimum of 18 months and millions of dollars, I just need deeper pockets behind me to do business I used to be able to accomplish with resources I could put together myself." Big projects are the domain of big organizations, especially in an era of lower leverage.

At the same time, large lenders are more cautious in the greater regulatory scrutiny they face. If you are designated a systemically important financial institution (SIFI), you face hurdles that limit activities that might have been your norm in the years before the global financial crisis.

As the historically more powerful banks are now more regulation-constrained, community and regional banks are more active. A Midwest banker with a regional footprint felt his SIFI-designated competitors were somewhat handicapped by capital surcharges, while the community and smaller banks were being encouraged to lend as a way to promote macroeconomic growth. However, he noted that "the smaller banks are

being stretched for yield" by the sheer volume of capital. "Are they being paid for the risk they are taking?"

The community lenders themselves must watch their portfolios so they don't grow to a size that tips them into more regulations. Right now, those banks are a go-to source of development financing, and local developers are increasingly knocking on the doors of those banks for projects in the $20 million to $50 million range. Many real estate projects are right in that size class.

What it means—and what the trend looks like going forward—is another instance of how granularity is the texture of the industry. Or, to change the metaphor, the sharpness of your picture is really dependent on the density of its pixels. Success will be a matter of "high resolution" operations in 2016 and beyond.

9. We Raised the Capital; Now, What Do We Do with It?

The flow of capital into U.S. real estate continues to increase. Total acquisition volume for the 12 months ending June 30, 2015, was $497.4 billion, up 24.6 percent year-over-year. While this pace of growth is probably not sustainable, investors across the board (with the exception of the government-sponsored enterprises [GSEs]) are anticipated to have capital availability in 2016 that is equal to or greater than 2015 levels. With pricing already near record levels in a number of markets and property types, where will this new capital be invested?

- **Additional markets.** Capital is expected to begin to flow more freely to 18-hour cities, as discussed in Trend 1.

Exhibit 1-16 Potential Investment Universe, by Market Classification

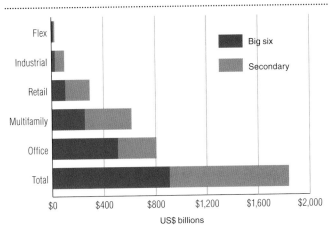

Legend: Big six, Secondary

Categories (top to bottom): Flex, Industrial, Retail, Multifamily, Office, Total

US$ billions (axis: $0, $400, $800, $1,200, $1,600, $2,000)

Sources: CoStar and PwC.

Exhibit 1-17 U.S. Sales of Large Commercial Properties

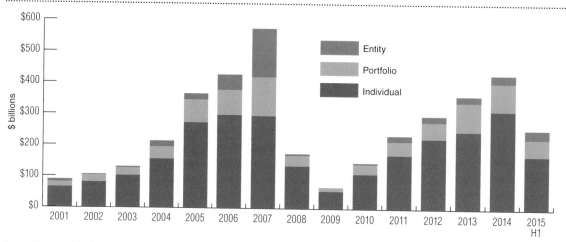

Source: Real Capital Analytics.

Note: Based on independent reports of properties and portfolios $2.5 million and greater. Before 2005, RCA primarily captured sales valued at $5 million and above.

- **Alternative assets.** The definition of what constitutes real estate is likely to continue expanding. We have seen the expansion of REITs to include cell towers and outdoor advertising. Retailers and restaurants continue to look at unlocking the potential value in their real estate holdings so that they can devote the capital to their core business. Discovering a way for private investors to creatively and profitably invest in infrastructure could also expand the real estate–related investable universe.

- **Old is new again.** Renovation and redevelopment are not new concepts, but the fervor with which the market is embracing older space is making the market consider a wider range of potential investments. Reports from markets about the popularity of office space housed in rehabbed industrial space demanding rents above new Class A product serve only to support this idea. Much of this is related to the changing work environment discussed in Trend 3. Other uses for obsolete urban industrial space include "last mile" distribution facilities and even urban farming as discussed in Trend 7.

- **Alternative property types.** Institutional investor interest begins to expand to alternative property types that to date have been dominated by a more limited investor set. Property types such as medical office and senior housing could potentially see a benefit from changing demographics. Data centers and lab space may be positioned to be in demand due to technological changes.

Real estate will not be standing pat.

We see greater inclination to order off the full menu, rather than taking *prix fixe* options, a continuation of our observation in *Emerging Trends 2015* that "everyone is in everyone else's business." As investors seek to balance capital conservation with capital growth, it will be harder to characterize investors as exclusively core, value-add, or opportunistic. Rather, the providers and the intermediaries of real estate capital are looking at the entire spectrum, moving deeper into the geography and the property-type mix available in the United States.

A broker with a large national office practice told us, "It is an extremely competitive market for placing capital." That competition is driving money more and more into a discovery process, a process many describe using the term *granularity*. Drilling down into markets and submarkets, working with smaller assets within the larger markets, specialized property types—these are all examples of the search to identify thriving niche opportunities. As that broker also remarked in his interview, "More capital will be moving into the 'middle' market—assets in the $10 million to $25 million range in primary, secondary, and tertiary markets. This market is attractive to those managing family wealth and other investors." As much as the big players capture headline attention, there is plenty of room—and plenty of capital—at work off the front pages of the news.

10. Return of the Human Touch

We are passing from the "dazzle" era of technology and big data, to the more difficult tasks of wise application. The idea that expertise in slicing and dicing numbers is the skill most needed in real estate financial analysis has been exposed as inadequate. The global financial crisis did not get triggered because of a lack of mathematical aptitude. The folks who got us all into trouble knew math just fine. What they lacked was the good judgment to foresee consequences and the conscientious determination to prudently manage to standards other than short-run profits. For such tasks, computers are of little help.

The industry is trending toward more intensively active management, even by "beta" investors building institutional portfolios. Investment by algorithm, with equations constructed on variations in historical data, can be out of date in the blink of an eye in a fast-changing world. In business, the element of trust—an intangible but real factor—matters most in difficult times. Those who have had to cope with severe dislocation get this. That is why being a "fiduciary" counts for so much.

Risk management of hacking issues also is of critical concern in a more internet-dependent business world. With both business and government computer systems vulnerable, attention to cybersecurity will penetrate ever more deeply into the real estate business. This will be even more important as the "internet of things" grows more prevalent. Can a hacker take control of your car? Of your HVAC system? Of your financial reporting? You bet. Real estate attention to countermeasures will be on the rise.

In a world mesmerized by what can be downloaded onto a smartphone, we've run the danger of falling in love with our toys. The next step is a greater skepticism of "apps" without the management of "human judgment interface." Attention to individual decision making is needed as much as ever. Could we call this trend "the return of the humans"?

Issues to Watch

Listing the top trends affecting real estate in the near-term and mid-term future can hardly cover all the ground worth the industry's attention. Physical, financial, regulatory, demographic, and social forces are much too complex for that. So we think it worthwhile to point out a few other topics to keep on the radar screen.

1. **Interest rates.** The era of rising rates now appears to be launched, after years of anticipation. Agreement is widespread that the variables are the degree and timing of change. Of course, the "black swan" factor of unforeseen events always exists—especially any economic or geopolitical occurrence raising the specter of deflation, which could postpone the anticipated period of rising Treasury rates, and those rates benchmarked against Treasuries. The underlying question is how the generation whose entire business career has been shaped by a low-interest-rate environment will respond to the upward movement in the price of money. Will higher rates alter behaviors, to what degree, and at what threshold? Keep an eye on such questions.

2. **Water.** The historic drought afflicting the western United States has brought cascading impacts to the region—and to the nation. The prodigiously productive California agricultural industry is also a tremendously thirsty activity. As irrigation has become more problematic and costly, so too have food prices for crops ranging from almonds and artichokes to pistachios and raisins. Some signs of declining farmland values are being seen as output is constrained. But agriculture is far from the only economic sector affected. Semiconductor plants require enormous amounts of water for operations, as do the "cloud storage" data centers now so integral to the internet. Even the snow-making machines at ski resorts—which become even more essential when Mother Nature is uncooperative in providing the white stuff—draw large quantities of water to keep the region's resort and recreation businesses humming. Wildfires, meanwhile, have scorched

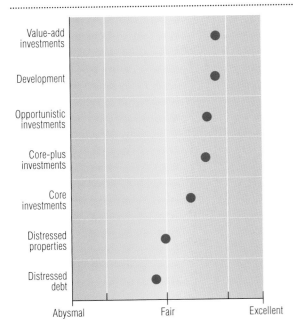

Exhibit 1-18 Prospects by Investment Category/Strategy, 2016

Value-add investments
Development
Opportunistic investments
Core-plus investments
Core investments
Distressed properties
Distressed debt

Abysmal — Fair — Excellent

Source: *Emerging Trends in Real Estate* surveys.

Note: Based on U.S. respondents only.

more than 87 million acres in the past decade—a land area equivalent to the state of New Mexico—not only in forests, but also in residential communities throughout the West. Cities whose economic energy has been driven by population increases must confront limits on growth that are defined by water availability and cost. Although a strong El Niño for the winter of 2015–2016 is forecast to bring much-needed rain, the water deficit west of the 100th Meridian is a factor that real estate should watch closely in the years ahead.

3. **Generation X.** Caught between the baby boomers and the millennials, both of whom get outsized attention, gen Xers (those born from 1965 to 1980) are now understood as those needed to take the reins of business. They are in a good position, in a way, as they are the ones whom the boomers should be grooming for management succession. But they came of age in the aftermath of the savings-and-loan crisis, in dire times for real estate. Few came into the business during the early 1990s, and even fewer have the benefit of real estate graduate education. Watch for the implications for leadership in the industry going forward.

4. **The Fair Housing Act and the Affordability Crisis.** The Supreme Court has affirmed that local communities can take legal action to address disparities in housing, even if they are the unintentional result of actions rather than conscious discrimination. The U.S. Department of Housing and Urban Development (HUD) is requiring local communities to "affirmatively further" equal housing opportunity, with communities risking losing out on federal housing funding for noncompliance. This could alter where affordable housing is built, and where households in need of such housing may move. When asked to identify barriers to affordable housing production, *Emerging Trends* survey respondents list local regulation, development costs (labor and materials), and land costs at the top of the list; NIMBY-ism also was cited as a factor. Watch for a heated debate on multifamily development against the background the U.S. Supreme Court and HUD rulings.

5. **Good jobs and income mobility.** As we move into the era of increased labor shortages discussed in *Emerging Trends in Real Estate 2015*, one great challenge will be planning for career paths. This includes succession planning for executives in the boomer generation, who need to groom gen-X leaders, who are relatively fewer in number. More generally, managers need to prepare for the era when new gen-Y workers are outnumbered by those retiring. Increasingly, that will mean that promoting from within will make more economic sense than competing for outside talent. And with employers

already lamenting the difficulty of finding workers with the right skills, worker development has to be part of the solution. For many employers, that is going to mean rethinking the college degree as an appropriate threshold for qualification. Such a trend is beginning in the blue-collar sector, but it will eventually filter into white-collar jobs. Watch an initiative called GoBuild, a collaboration among trade associations like the Associated General Contractors, labor unions, local economic developers, and vocational and technical training schools. Apprenticeship programs are combined with "earn while you learn" training. Importantly, the education component starts *before* college. Better to have incomes than student debt, many feel. Keep an eye on this movement, which is being led by states like Georgia and Alabama.

Expected Best Bets for 2016

Emerging Trends survey respondents and interviewees expressed their informed opinions about "what to do to prosper in the year ahead." Here are some of their most salient observations.

Go to Key Secondary Markets

Price resistance is an issue for gateway markets. Secondary markets, especially 18-hour cities, are emerging as great relative value propositions. Such markets are "hip, urban, walkable, and attractive to the millennials" while providing better future opportunities for rising net income and appreciation than the 24-hour city markets that led the post–financial crisis real estate recovery.

These secondary markets (think Austin, Portland, Nashville, Charlotte, and similar cities) boast lower costs of living—particularly in housing—and strong growth potential. Value-add investors can access multiple sources of real estate financing from insurance companies, CMBS lenders, private equity firms, and cross-border investors. With this positive liquidity profile and socioeconomic fundamentals, asset selection in secondary markets should pay off as a 2016 strategy.

Take a Deep Dive into the Data

The era of big data can be a blessing or a curse. The avalanche of numbers pouring down each day creates a daunting challenge to separate "the signal from the noise." Having a clear strategy is the key: a well-defined set of criteria for property characteristics, submarket qualities, and demand segments helps the investment focus. Deals that meet specific investment objectives will vary business by business. One size does not fit all.

Once the filtering process is accomplished, the skill set of experienced real estate professionals takes over: analysis of operating statements and rent rolls, assessing cap-ex needs—

Exhibit 1-20 **Metropolitan Mobility by Generation, 2013–2014**

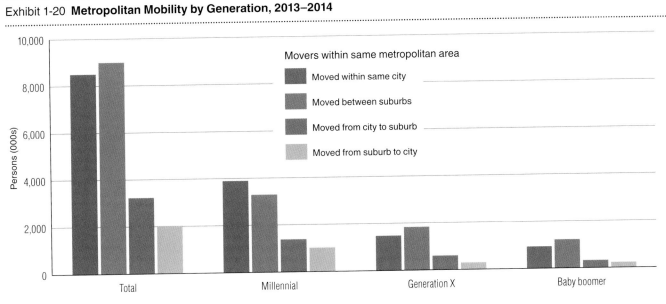

Source: U.S. Census Bureau.

nitty-gritty asset management. The amount of information available at the submarket and property levels surpasses even the greediest wish list of a generation ago. The advantage belongs not to those who can **get the data** (pretty much everybody), but those who can **use the data.**

Middle-Income Multifamily Housing

The real estate industry has a chance to provide creative answers for "the excluded middle" of American households. There's a good chance to do solid business, too. The upper end of the multifamily housing market is saturated with product, sometimes at ridiculously low cap rates. That should turn development attention to midpriced units in or near growing employment centers to find a competitive edge. Affordable housing can be a viable enterprise.

Governments need to help: equity supports, middle-class tax benefits, and incentives for upgrading dilapidated older housing are all in the public interest. The luxury market is thin, and picked over. The heavily subsidized low end is complicated, low-margin, and politicized. But millions of households need mid- to higher-density housing in the middle-income range, in urban and suburban settings. That's opportunity writ large for those able to target it.

Plan Your Parking for Change

The advent of autonomous vehicles, the shift to walkability and transit proximity as a location preference, and the concomi-

tant decline in driving licenses among the young are forcing a hard look at conventional parking ratios. This is not just about suburban surface parking, although there are bound to be reuse opportunities in that sector. It is about rethinking the way that user preferences, new technologies, and urban form interact.

Live/work/play downtowns need fewer parking slots per 1,000 square feet of office space or per multifamily unit. Developments in the path of planned mass transit should consider temporary versus permanent parking needs. Planning and zoning requirements should be revisited in light of the emerging trends in transportation and land use.

Go Long on REITs Priced Substantially below NAV

REITs live in parallel universes—the real estate markets and the stock markets. The occasional mismatch between valuations in these two arenas can lead to substantial arbitrage opportunities, and 2016 is shaping up to be one of those periods. Volatility and price correction in stocks have caught REITs in a more generalized downdraft. But improved property market fundamentals have bolstered the value of the sticks-and-bricks

In a period of low cap rates, REITs are high-dividend equity instruments. Those looking for low leverage will find it on REIT balance sheets. Search out REITs with solid "A" properties, especially if they are in the 24-hour or 18-hour markets, for a great combination of offense (alpha returns due to pricing arbitrage) and defense (high-quality buildings in top markets).

Capital Markets

"There's an investor or a lender for every viable deal."

Real estate is the meeting place for all three forms of capital: physical capital, financial capital, and human capital. When real estate people speak about capital, though, the rule is "follow the money." The discussion moves on many levels: Sources of equity and debt capital. Strategies. Motivation. Pricing and returns. Timing and structure. Expectations. Risk.

Capital markets and real estate markets are in the minds of a much broader public than just the property development, investment, and service industry. The nonfiction best-seller list has seen titles such as Hernando de Soto's *The Mystery of Capital* (2000) and Thomas Piketty's *Capital in the Twenty-First Century* (2014). The very nature of real estate projects makes them public events and subjects of reports in the print and electronic media. International investment—whether in a Manhattan condominium, a suburban office park in Houston,

or a mixed-use development in Los Angeles's central business district (CBD)—invariably makes headlines. When a televised presidential debate explores the strategic use of bankruptcy by a casino owner, with 24 million viewers tuned in, a new level of public awareness has been reached.

The big picture is this: In many ways, it appears that worldwide capital accumulation has rebounded fully from the global financial crisis. The recovery of capital around the globe has been extremely uneven. And the sorting-out process has favored the United States and the real estate industry, affecting prices, yields, and risk management for all participants in the market.

In the view of a Wall Street investment adviser, **"There is going to be a long wave of continued capital allocation towards our business,** even though interest rates in the U.S. are defi-

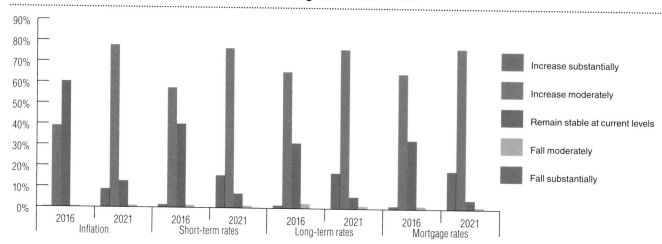

Exhibit 2-1 **Anticipated Inflation and Interest Rate Changes in 2016 and 2021**

Source: *Emerging Trends in Real Estate 2016* surveys.

Note: Based on U.S. respondents only.

Exhibit 2-2 Availability of Capital for Real Estate in 2016

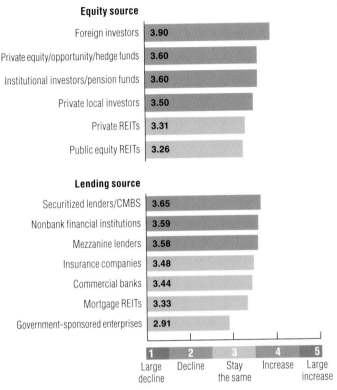

Equity source

Source	Rating
Foreign investors	3.90
Private equity/opportunity/hedge funds	3.60
Institutional investors/pension funds	3.60
Private local investors	3.50
Private REITs	3.31
Public equity REITs	3.26

Lending source

Source	Rating
Securitized lenders/CMBS	3.65
Nonbank financial institutions	3.59
Mezzanine lenders	3.58
Insurance companies	3.48
Commercial banks	3.44
Mortgage REITs	3.33
Government-sponsored enterprises	2.91

1	2	3	4	5
Large decline	Decline	Stay the same	Increase	Large increase

Source: *Emerging Trends in Real Estate* surveys.

Note: Based on U.S. respondents only.

Exhibit 2-3 Moody's/RCA Commercial Property Price Index, by Major/Nonmajor Markets

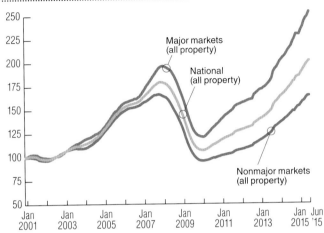

Sources: Moody's and Real Capital Analytics.

Notes: Major markets are defined here as Boston, Chicago, Los Angeles, San Francisco, New York City, and Washington, D.C. The Moody's/RCA Commercial Property Price Index is based on repeat-sales transactions that occurred anytime through the month before the current report. Updated August 2015; data through June 2015.

nitely going to go up at some point [and] even though you see more supply in most of the product categories."

The close-up picture is this: America's real estate market contains many niches, with tremendous diversity of participants and asset types. One size definitely does not fit all. That diversity is a key strength because it promotes liquidity, price discovery, and opportunities to enter or exit the market.

Even in terms of an industry-wide concern such as regulation, impacts will vary considerably. Reaction to rules on banking, including Dodd-Frank and Basel III, is changing the lending landscape. **Smaller investors, meanwhile, care a lot about 1031 exchanges and the potential impact of proposed legislation limiting or eliminating the tax deferral benefit of like-kind exchanges.** Many developers, meanwhile, have been using capital made available under the EB-5 program, which has "pretty much become mainstream," according to a West Coast investment manager. (EB-5 grants a visa that can lead to permanent residency in the United States for those mak-

ing eligible investments there. Those investments must create at least ten jobs for U.S. workers, and amounts are set at a $1 million minimum, or $500,000 for rural or high-unemployment market areas.)

Those on-the-ground differences make it imperative to look at the specific trends and conditions shaping the equity and debt participants in the real estate capital markets for 2016 and beyond.

The Debt Sector

The 2016 *Emerging Trends* survey indicates a dramatic pivot point in refinancing expectations. A year ago, 35 percent of the respondents anticipated an undersupply of such capital. Now, 35 percent say they expect an oversupply of money for refinancing. ("In balance" responses are roughly the same.) The 2016 refinancing expectation resembles what the acquisition financing projections were a year ago.

If oversupply for acquisition debt was the consensus last year, respondents think that 2016's environment will be "even more so." But, for development, debt capital is forecast to remain disciplined.

With the exception of the government-sponsored enterprises (GSEs), debt capital availability is expected to grow at a moder-

Exhibit 2-4 Debt Underwriting Standards Forecast for the United States

	Less rigorous	Remain the same	More rigorous
2016	35.4%	51.7%	12.9%
2015	45.7%	44.7%	9.6%
2014	43.3%	39.4%	17.4%
2013	19.6%	41.5%	39.1%
2012	31.9%	35.1%	33.0%
2011	29.8%	29.2%	41.0%

Source: *Emerging Trends in Real Estate* surveys.
Note: Based on U.S. respondents only.

Exhibit 2-5 Equity Underwriting Standards Forecast for the United States

	Less rigorous	Remain the same	More rigorous
2016	34.0%	52.4%	13.6%
2015	41.4%	47.5%	11.1%
2014	30.7%	50.8%	18.5%
2013	19.6%	50.7%	29.7%
2012	22.8%	46.7%	30.5%
2011	26.6%	40.6%	32.8%

Source: *Emerging Trends in Real Estate* surveys.
Note: Based on U.S. respondents only.

ate pace from all sources. That could signal that this recovery is hitting its mature phase.

The majority of survey respondents are not suggesting further easing in debt underwriting standards, and the number expecting less rigorous loan requirements dropped by about ten percentage points compared with the prior year. As noted last year, lenders' spreads have been compressed almost to the point where the following critical question assumes paramount importance: "Are we being paid for the risk we are taking?" If spreads are thin, risk must be managed in other elements of the deal—most particularly, in the loan-to-value ratio where the borrower's "skin in the game" has had to increase. Intense competition exists among the lenders for the "A-quality" deals in the market, and it is here that we may see some underwriting flexibility to secure core properties for the balance sheet.

The expectation that a regime of rising interest rates is upon us and will shape mortgage and construction loan pricing in the 2016–2021 period is virtually universal. In the short run, recent past experience about Fed caution leads 30 to 40 percent to anticipate general interest rate stability for 2016 itself.

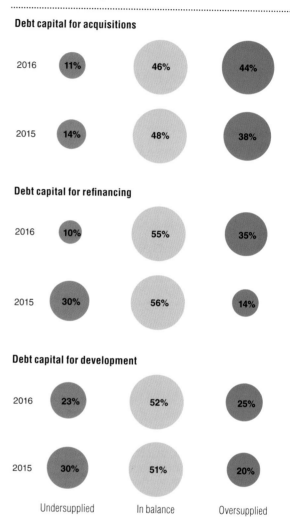

Exhibit 2-6 Real Estate Capital Market Balance Forecast, 2016 versus 2015

Debt capital for acquisitions

	Undersupplied	In balance	Oversupplied
2016	11%	46%	44%
2015	14%	48%	38%

Debt capital for refinancing

	Undersupplied	In balance	Oversupplied
2016	10%	55%	35%
2015	30%	56%	14%

Debt capital for development

	Undersupplied	In balance	Oversupplied
2016	23%	52%	25%
2015	30%	51%	20%

Source: *Emerging Trends in Real Estate* surveys.
Note: Based on U.S. respondents only.

Sharp disagreement exists among *Emerging Trends* interviewees about the potential for disruptions as rates rise, often tied to the expected degree and pace of the rate increases. Those fearing the worst echo a seasoned commercial lender who told us, "I think if we get more than 50 basis points' movement by February, people are going to be reeling. Everybody thinks they can get through the eye of the needle right at the end. I think an interest rate surprise to the upside is going to throw people for a loop." In a more sanguine perspective, a private equity executive notes, "Rising rates are generally good for CRE [commercial real estate]. The last five cycles show high correlation between rising interest rates and higher CRE prices."

Following is a look at the various categories of lenders, and the outlook for debt capital from each in 2016 and beyond.

Commercial Banks

Regulation is biting. Dodd-Frank requirements are particularly constraining big banks, in concert with Consumer Protection Act provisions. And the Basel III rules about "high-volatility commercial real estate" loans expose bank lenders to higher capital reserving requirements for acquisition, development, and construction lending that are anything but extremely conservative. One banker interviewed noted that "banks will need to rebuild their systems to accommodate these new rules" and believed that it would reduce the volume of lending and/or raise its price.

Others, however, think that this is exactly the point. Disciplined lending by banks that have strong capital foundations are essential not only for solid real estate market performance, but also for the well-being of the financial system itself. As the head of an international institutional investor remarked, "The bubble was created by overlending." Even though experience teaches that the next recession will not look like the last one, it is in no one's interest to have a replay of the global financial crisis.

On the ground, banks are doing business. A lender with a national commercial real estate program says, "Regulation is largely good, but requires a lot of work," but that the result is that new deals are not "priced to perfection." There is cushion against risk. This lender cited loan-to-values (LTVs) of 75 percent with partial recourse, but 65 percent or lower with no recourse. Nevertheless, spreads have been reduced, which is a clear sign of competition for real estate lending among the banks.

An executive with an analytics firm focused on the debt markets reflected, "Smaller banks are back in business and have resolved most of their problems. **Extend-and-pretend actually worked pretty well for banks.** It allowed banks to address problems over time as the markets recovered, rather than using a mark-to-market approach."

One Midwest developer/owner said, "Credit is very available. Banks are becoming more like the life companies, with longer loans available. I have found commercial banks very accommodating." The competition is cutting both ways, apparently, since a developer in the Southeast reported accessing construction funding from an insurance company willing to then provide the takeout financing.

CMBS

A West Coast consultant's forecast of $125 billion to $135 billion in new commercial mortgage–backed securities (CMBS) issu-

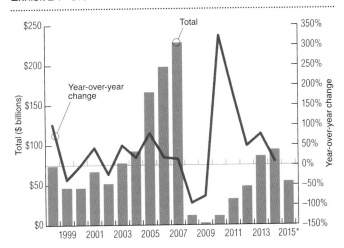

Exhibit 2-7 U.S. CMBS Issuance

Source: *Commercial Mortgage Alert.*

* Total through June 30, 2015.

ance in 2016 is in line with the trend of recovery in securitized lending. He believes CMBS is "a financing source that's very valuable for commodity real estate and some single-asset real estate." An investment adviser described such structured finance as "very efficient for secondary and tertiary markets," a key attribute as investment activity accelerates beyond the high-priced gateway markets in the years ahead. An analyst specializing in the structured-debt world says, "CMBS is no longer in a dominant position, which is probably good for the market."

Not only past history, but also going-forward concerns about credit quality are the critical issues for CMBS in the year ahead. An institutional investor cautioned, "The CMBS market is where folks are really looking as to whether that sector will have more discipline or not. So far it's the sector where we're seeing the most erosion of underwriting, mostly in conduit loans." He identifies as concerns "rating agency [independence], loan-to-value [levels], and percent of loans with interest only are certainly objective measures that show that there's been erosion in underwriting."

One important area of ambiguity is in the alignment of the interests of the originators of CMBS and the purchasers of the bonds. One post-crash reform is the practice of originators holding some of the risk on their own books.

Conduit lenders are looking to provide capital for deals that are good, but not so pristine as to pass muster as portfolio assets to be held on the books for liquidity ratio and capital reserving purposes. But, to be marketable as a securities issuance, the great bulk of CMBS needs to be rated as "investment-grade." So the AAA tranche is the key for institutional demand for the bonds. Spreads for that piece have been widening, tempering the profitability of the issuance as a greater risk premium is demanded by bond purchasers. "At the first-loss position," says the chief investment officer of a commercial mortgage bank, "B-piece buyers are becoming more selective on the loans they will take because they are concerned about the underwriting having worsened in the past 12 to 24 months."

The *caveat emptor* lesson has been learned, and the greater discipline imposed by the CMBS bond-buying community should help the performance of the instruments over time. But it also is the reason why issuance is highly unlikely to achieve the $200 billion–plus levels seen before the global financial crisis.

One final story to watch in 2016–2018: These are the years when the "refi cliff" was due to inflict a death blow to the CMBS industry, as securities issued at the peak of the frothy market a decade ago came due and payable. Of course, the recovery of prices since 2011 has taken the most dire risks off the table. But there is still a quantity of CMBS backed by assets in commercial real estate markets that have not seen full price recovery. **The Asset Securitization Report issued in early 2015 estimated that 20 percent of the $300 billion to be refinanced over three years would require additional capital.** So a threat of haircuts for some bondholders still exists.

That threat may be mitigated by the overall higher level of liquidity in the markets—both debt and equity. If you must sell or recapitalize property, now is a good time to do so, and the private markets may provide the exit strategy that the public debt markets will not.

From within the industry, an appreciation of the role of CMBS in the entire panoply of debt finance has taken hold. An association executive observes, "The industry is starting to 'ask the questions' regarding overbuilding, overvaluation, and so forth, which is a 'good and different thing' from prior cycles." It should be remembered that CMBS is just a 20-year-old market. Learning from experience is entirely appropriate.

Insurance Companies

Perhaps no source of debt capital is exploiting the surge of demand for commercial real estate funding more shrewdly than the life companies. Even as they expand their volume (a 6 percent increase year-over-year as of the first quarter of 2015), there has been a strategic focus on asset selection for the long term. This, of course, is a textbook move, sifting out lower-quality

applications, respecting portfolio allocations, and managing toward satisfying actuarial liabilities.

Even when we hear of life companies providing development financing, an overarching rationale is at work: positioning toward providing the permanent financing on a desired "core" asset.

Federal Reserve data show that life insurance companies have $305.7 billion in commercial mortgages outstanding, a 12.7 percent market share that has remained basically stable over the past year, in line with our expectations in *Emerging Trends 2015*. This measure of the insurance industry's market share excludes multifamily holdings, which add another $57 billion to their balance sheets, a 5.6 percent share of this property type. So the strategic aim has not targeted expanding market share at a time when borrower demand is robust. Rather, it has been to secure assets that will perform well across cycles. The enviable default/delinquency record of the insurers during the global financial crisis demonstrates the wisdom of such attention to relative value, and it is one of the reasons that regulators have not spotlighted this sector to the degree they have zeroed in on commercial and investment banks.

What are the policies and procedures supporting such performance, and the underlying financing philosophy that borrowers can expect in bringing deals to the life companies in 2016?

A typical major life company platform prefers holding the senior debt position, with express limits on the amount of subordinated debt permitted. Twenty- to 30-year amortization is standard, with interest-only loans considered if the LTV is below 65 percent. Even when participating in structured lending ventures—colending or allowing subordinated debt—the life companies retain decision-making rights, and require institutional-grade property and sponsorship.

While geographic diversification is a consideration, insurance company lenders prefer primary markets and a handful of secondary markets. There is no drive to be everywhere. Consequently, the life companies can comfortably commit to very large mortgage investments. This creates efficiency in the deployment of capital as well as staff resources. The big life insurance companies have been at this a long time, and have refined their game nicely. All in all, the life companies seem to have little inclination to match the expansion of lending at regional and community banks. There is a willingness to sacrifice market share to preserve loan quality. There are enough qualified potential borrowers to satisfy underwriting standards while funding the insurers' allocations for commercial real estate.

Keeping future defaults at a *de minimis* level is an objective of paramount importance. Conservativism in lending is the overriding investment philosophy, for sure.

That conservatism is a factor to take into account in understanding the very thin spreads in insurance company lending. The spread is not only profit margin, but also payment for risk. Managing risk at the asset level by strict underwriting, and at the portfolio level by sophisticated diversification, helps keep the appropriate risk premium for life company lenders lower than that for those taking more idiosyncratic risk in their mortgage products.

REIT Debt

"The trend for REITs is evolutionary rather than a distinct break in pattern. This market has been steady and should remain that way," says a noted Wall Street analyst following this sector.

Publicly traded REITs have access to debt capital in the corporate finance sector, sources that are not typically available at the property level per se. REITs have been successfully issuing commercial paper, for instance, for short-term capital needs. This has supplemented their use of lines of credit, and the commercial paper is often backed by the company's line of credit. This is a useful bridge financing tool, as long as the REIT's funds from operations (FFO) will support repayment. The rating agencies monitor this closely.

Such access to debt in the public markets is likely to be more important, as bankers interviewed suggest that large loans to large REITs are going to be limited by the tighter regulations in the banking sector.

As a provider of debt capital, it is the 40-plus mortgage REITs (market capitalization of about $70 billion) that supplement the banks, life companies, CMBS, and private debt funds in funneling mortgage money to the real estate investment markets. Mortgage REIT (M-REIT) assets are vastly weighted toward the residential sector, and they have been contributors to the strong performance of the multifamily arena through the purchase of U.S. agency (Fannie Mae and Freddie Mac) bonds during the period of conservancy that began in 2008. The market for agency debt is very large—over $6 trillion—and mortgage REITs have about a 5 percent share.

The most recent Federal Reserve data (issued June 11, 2015) show mortgage REITs holding $166.2 billion in commercial property mortgages, or roughly half the level of the life insurance companies. This was down about $5 billion from year-end 2014, indicating net sales and lower production by the M-REITs.

The National Association of Real Estate Investment Trusts (NAREIT) Index for M-REITs was down 2.2 percent in total returns year-to-date through July 2015, compared with a Standard & Poor's 500 gain of 3.4 percent. The holdings of mortgage REITs are fixed-income assets and hence are particularly sensitive to movements in interest rates. Since the public markets are anticipatory, reflecting the expectation of rising interest rates into 2016, the year ahead is unlikely to see this segment of the debt markets expanding aggressively.

Borrowers seeking to access M-REIT debt capacity should anticipate a preference for variable-rate instruments and a requirement for higher yield-to-maturity coupon rates. For those borrowers willing and able to work with such terms, the M-REITs may be a more flexible, if more expensive, source of mortgage money than either the regulated banking sector or the core-asset-oriented life companies in the near future. Borrowers can be expected to fall into the value-add and opportunistic buckets of investment style, financing turnaround acquisitions, as well as development. If borrowers are willing to take on (and hedge) the interest rate risk, M-REITs can price loans more competitively than if they hold that risk as lenders.

Bespoke Lending

"Debt funds are growing like dandelions," one *Emerging Trends* interviewee said. "There is more mezzanine debt out there than there are deals," said another, "and they are high-priced." A national-scale investor/owner remarked, "Private debt funds can make loans outside of the Basel III–regulated environment. Protections against bad actors is an expense; it's not free."

Here is where the complex ecology of the debt space benefits the market as a whole: Evolution is all about successful adaptation. In the early phase of the global financial crisis, many investors saw the Resolution Trust Corporation era as the model to be emulated. These investors were disappointed as fire-sale pricing failed to materialize. In the end, it is hard to fault the strategy of patience in 2009–2012. But it has left a residue of capital seeking placement.

Space in the capital stack is opening up as larger institutional lenders are increasingly sticking with safe loans on top-quality assets. **A lot of U.S. real estate sits below that top tier, falling either into the value-add category or in secondary or tertiary markets currently off the radar screen of the most risk-averse lenders. That could prove to be a great opportunity** for bespoke lenders if the economy and the property markets continue to improve in the next few years.

For example, some of the vintage CMBS maturing in 2016–2018 may require gap financing from the private sector debt funds, as anticipated by one institutional asset manager. As noted earlier in this chapter, this could represent as much as 20 percent of the securities requiring refinancing.

The reluctance of senior lenders to accommodate subordinated debt in the capital stack creates another opening. Private debt funds may find themselves repositioning their approach to favor investment in the preferred equity space. That is a comparable spot in the capital stack, between common equity and senior debt. The large banks can count preferred equity favorably in LTV reporting, while an overall increase in property indebtedness plays poorly in reporting to the regulators.

The trend of bespoke lending—custom-tailoring for borrowers without off-the-rack needs—is likely to accelerate in the second half of the decade. This is partly because of the need to play offense, in responding to borrowers' needs for flexibility and timing. We found at least one pension fund manager looking to supply such short-term needs, in return for a quicker return on capital invested, for example. But it is also partly responding to the institutional lenders' increasing obligation to play defense in a more regulated lending environment.

Overall, the outlook for the quantity and quality of lending in 2016 looks good. If volume is rising, this is not at the expense of basic underwriting. As one interviewee put it, **"If debt is a little less fantastic, this is a good thing."** Loan applicants may find accessing debt a bit easier next year than last, but no lender is indiscriminately pushing money out the door.

The key is for the borrower to candidly evaluate what is being presented and then to search the whole lending field for the most likely source of mortgage funding. The money is there, and someone is specializing in what each borrower needs. The variable, of course, is pricing. But real estate debt in 2016 will still be very cheap by historical standards, and borrowers should look to take advantage of that while the opportunity exists.

The Equity Sector

The United States has long boasted the largest, deepest, and most diverse real estate market on the planet. That remains true. But a question not often considered needs to be raised: Are we big enough to absorb the volume of investment capital directed our way without undergoing—again—disruptive change?

Much of the industry's trend later in the decade will be shaped by investor behaviors in 2016. This could be a pivotal year for

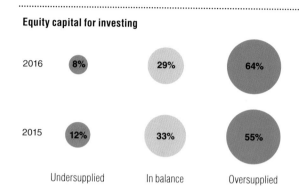

Exhibit 2-8 **Real Estate Capital Market Balance Forecast, 2016 versus 2015**

Equity capital for investing

	Undersupplied	In balance	Oversupplied
2016	8%	29%	64%
2015	12%	33%	55%

Source: *Emerging Trends in Real Estate* surveys.
Note: Based on U.S. respondents only.

real estate. The concept of "path dependence" suggests that the experience of the coming year—considered to include greater movement to secondary markets, greater attention to value-add assets, and the expectation of an extension of the U.S. economic expansion—advantages real estate vis-à-vis other investments in the United States and abroad.

Here is where the size, depth, and diversity of the real estate markets can play to advantage. The varying equity sources have distinct capacities, motivations, return requirements, and appetite for risk. It is not as though there is a single ocean of equity capital to be deployed. Rather, there are streams of capital flowing to the markets. That is plural "streams" and plural "markets." The most urgent questions are whether and how those streams of capital will stay within their banks, nourishing rather than flooding their target markets.

Let's be clear at the outset: The recovery of transaction volumes and pricing to pre–financial crisis levels, especially in the gateway markets, is not *prima facie* evidence of a bubble.

Much is different from a decade ago, not least the alteration in the amount of leverage in the market. Soaring leverage ratios are one of the hallmarks of bubble economies over the course of history, and both the real estate and banking industries have been assiduous in limiting that risk. This is critical, since the reduction of equity cushions sets the stage for equity extinction when cycles turn downward. The situation where lenders-in-possession are pushed to get troubled assets off their books can degrade to a free fall in prices, as the United States saw during the savings-and-loan crisis years, and again during the global financial crisis. Such a risk did not loom on the horizon as we prepared *Emerging Trends in Real Estate 2016*.

Exhibit 2-9 **Investment Prospects by Asset Class**

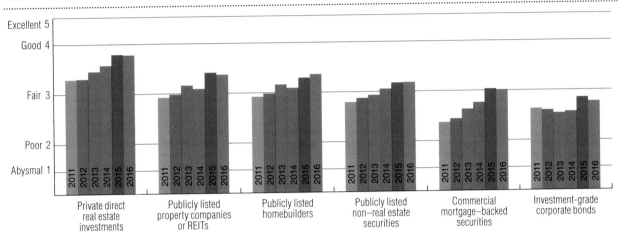

Source: *Emerging Trends in Real Estate* surveys.

Note: Based on U.S. respondents only.

Nevertheless, it is difficult to be entirely sunny when 64 percent of the survey respondents characterize the market as oversupplied with equity capital, and 34 percent believe that equity underwriting standards will become less rigorous in 2016. Balancing those figures is the mild retreat in the outlook for change in capital availability: still growing, but not so vigorously as in 2015.

This year, we find equity seeking to stay disciplined while dealing with a very competitive environment where all capital sources are geared up for transactions. **"In the current market situation, it is not hard to raise money; it is harder to find good deals, and hard competition when you do find one,"** said an investment banking interviewee.

Institutional Investors

It is in institutions' nature to have long memories. Experienced managers often ask themselves, "Have I seen this movie before?" Awareness of cyclical risk and opportunity is embedded in their DNA, yet there is a deep understanding that the next recession will probably not look like the last one. As long-term portfolio holders, the institutional investors who make up the National Council of Real Estate Investment Fiduciaries (NCREIF) data contributors are both fact- and theory-driven. They would have to be, with $426 billion invested in 6,863 properties as of the first quarter of 2015.

A Chicago-based investment consultant commented in his interview, "Real estate is just knocking on the door of the big-data era. That means more than just access to information; it means having systems and algorithms in place to sift out the

significance and guide decisions." That is where the institutional investors are today, and where they are headed tomorrow. Modern portfolio theory is just the foundation of institutional real estate investment operations. Besides running the numbers on portfolio allocations, there is still significant room for—indeed, a requirement for—good judgment.

With core properties in the gateway markets so richly priced, investors with deep pockets are searching for "alpha" using all investment styles, including value-add and opportunistic development. "You do have to 'dollar-cost-average' over the cycle," said the head of this firm, while affirming that one cannot effectively raise capital in a competitive market by being merely average. Even with holding periods typically longer than a single cycle, institutions are constantly culling their portfolios, taking profits (or cutting losses), and redeploying capital to improve yield. In the first half of 2015, for example, Real Capital Analytics tallied $55.7 billion in institutional acquisitions, and an even greater $74.5 billion in dispositions.

Another very large-scale institution stressed that core-only strategies in 2016 face pricing conditions reflecting 4 percent cap rates and a 6 percent internal rate of return (IRR) over ten years. Such returns do not satisfy actuarial requirements, and so this investor is, by its own reckoning, one of the nation's top four value-add investors, while still holding a huge core portfolio. In the value-add space, executives of that institution maintain, they can achieve yields that are in the 7 to 10 percent range while continuing to deploy their capital prudently. That means explicit criteria for the value-add underwriting, including a demonstrated case for cash-flow growth, in markets of proven liquidity, and leverage sufficiently low that a "worst-case scenario" still provides ample debt-service coverage.

The manager of a large state pension plan has his eye on the short term. "We are trying not to get into long-term investments. Instead, we are looking for investments where the capital returns sooner. The average life of investments should be three to five years." That is a real shift of perspective in the institutional space, and a telling indication that active management is a growing trend even in a sector heretofore known as "beta" investors.

Lastly, the institutions are acutely aware that their real estate investments do not exist in a vacuum. The head of equity investment strategy for a firm with some $40 billion of real estate under management warned, "In an increasingly volatile environment, whether it's weather or it's political instability and terrorism, pooling and sharing of risk is an important way to deal with uncertainty. That costs more. It's going to be an added cost of doing business, but I think it's more important than ever."

REITs

In the views of most *Emerging Trends* interviewees, the outlook for the REIT sector is bullish. "Business is as good as it's ever been," in the words of one REIT executive, and, "The market will be good for at least another two years, at a very conservative estimate." A fund manager concurs, adding, "REITs are buying everything because they have a cost-of-capital advantage." We see "nothing too frothy in REIT markets," according to one international institutional investor who suggests that **"REITs are the best vehicle for small real estate investors."**

A healthy REIT sector has a very positive impact on the U.S. property industry as a whole. It is a very large player, certainly, with the publicly traded REITs capitalized at $867 billion (as of July 31, 2015). REITs were net purchasers of real estate in the first half of 2015, to the tune of $8.4 billion, on gross acquisition volume of $37.9 billion. The public markets continue to provide capital, responding to an annualized total return of 16.9 percent, as reported by NAREIT this past summer.

A developer expressed it this way: "I consider the publicly traded REITs to be a little bit undervalued. I think the stock market as a whole is. When you sit there and say a space-sharing startup has the same capital value as a long-established and successful public REIT—I mean, come on, that's Wall Street hype. I'd rather own a share of the REIT at its price today than the 'unicorn,' if it were public."

An investment banker agrees: "Most [REIT] companies are probably trading at a discount of about 10 percent to net asset value,

depending on the sector. They're a little more hesitant to raise money now, but the money's there if they want it." That suggests that REITs can harvest profits by selective disposition in the short run, but should have plenty of capital for growth in 2016.

Investors have voted with their wallets in motivating REITs to "stick to their knitting," an interviewee observed. For the biggest REITs, that has meant moving up the quality chain and responding to the same changes in market preference as the institutional investors. "We used to want modern garden apartment complexes with highway frontage," remarked the CEO of one REIT, "but now we are only buying high-rise urban assets with great walk scores."

REITs live in the parallel universes of real estate and stock markets, and misalignments between the two domains constantly create tensions. Because of common perceptions on Wall Street, the rising interest rate environment of 2016 and 2017 that is expected is already putting downward pressure on share prices. If it turns out—as some others closer to the property market expect—that rising rates will be modulated in timing and degree in accord with employment change, the spread between net asset value (NAV) and share values may widen, but not necessarily so, since economic growth supported by job gains of 2.7 million to 3.0 million per year should eventually spur an equity market advance.

While all this is going on, some shareholders are pressing management at restaurant chains to monetize their real estate assets by entering the REIT IPO market. This will be a company-by-company set of choices, of course. Investors and management need to ask themselves some hard questions about the potential sales growth at the individual restaurant brand, and how much of the value of shares will depend upon locking the restaurants into long-term leases that, while providing steady dividends, will stress the low-end profit margins typical of mass-market food operations.

One repeated caution from the *Emerging Trends* interviewees concerned the smaller nontraded REIT sector due to concerns about illiquidity in the nontraded REITs and their lesser price transparency.

Lastly, the expansion of the REIT concept to forms of fixed assets beyond the traditional real estate property types may be an accelerating trend, if the regulators are flexible about qualifying assets. There already are REITs in power generation, distribution, and other forms of infrastructure. The public markets have often been creative in providing capital where needs emerge but are inadequately funded. There is reason to believe

Exhibit 2-10 **U.S. Buyers and Sellers: Net Acquisitions, by Source and Property Sector, 2Q 2014 to 2Q 2015**

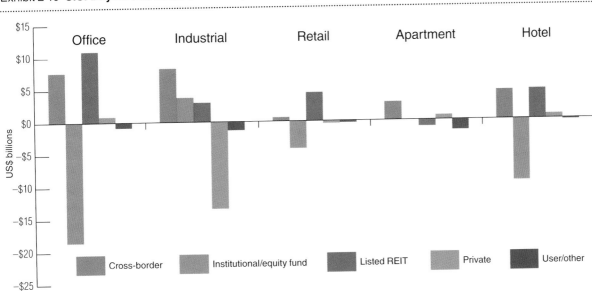

Source: Real Capital Analytics.

that the scope of the REIT industry has not yet fully expanded and that more growth lies ahead.

Private Equity

Since 2001, annual acquisition activity from private purchasers has grown faster than any other equity capital source (with the exception of cross-border investors). In the 12 months ending June 2015, private real estate investors bought $216 billion of U.S. property, or 43.5 percent of the total gross investment flow for that period. That compares with a 20.1 percent share for institutional investors, a 14.1 percent share for REITs, and an 11.7 percent share for international investors. This is clearly the major capital source for commercial property investment.

The trend should be for increasing activity. At least three reasons exist for such an outlook. First, **private equity capital is exceptionally nimble,** compared with capital sources where decisions must go through investment committee processes. Second, **private equity's reach is deeper into the broad U.S. market** since it is unencumbered by allocation decisions driven by portfolio considerations and by minimum deal size parameters typical of the largest investors.

Third, as a consequence, in an environment where core and core-plus assets are priced to perfection, **private equity can provide higher yields because it accesses more opportunistic investments.** If, as some think, many secondary and tertiary markets are approaching the point of real rent increases

and new development feasibility, the private funds should attract additional capital oriented to the higher yields in those "alpha-oriented" purchases. By the way, private equity investors are not alone in this perspective. A REIT executive with assets across the Sun Belt remarked, "We are looking for good growth, good tenant mix, rents moving upward in markets like Charlotte, Atlanta, Miami, Austin, and Phoenix."

One global investor argues, **"We are getting a better appreciation for how many great American cities there are—and how many American cities are doing great things—secondary cities showing hip, amenitized, urban, walkable, transit-oriented development."** The chief investment officer of one private equity firm says, "We have many investments in secondary markets. Markets with hospitals, universities, trade ports, and strong infrastructure generate higher quality of life, such as Austin, Charlotte, Charleston, Dallas, Denver, Nashville, and Raleigh."

Does that mean that private equity investors are at risk of overpromising and underdelivering? Not necessarily. Very few investors put much credibility in projections of 20 percent or higher returns these days. A banker specializing in the private equity space told us, "What I have seen over the last three years is a lowering of expectation on return." Generally, that means a realistic expectation in the low to mid-teens.

This is another reason to feel that the risk of an asset bubble in real estate is not especially high for 2016: across the board, the tendency for a more conservative financial structure is evident and investors think about return of capital as a primary consideration—and return on capital only once loss mitigation requirements are satisfied. This may be a powerful explanatory factor in low cap rates—even more powerful than the zero-interest-rate Fed policies that have been in place.

An interview with the head of a large equity fund featured a discussion of sifting through opportunity and risks across the entire spectrum of metropolitan economies and property types. The era of big data means that fewer secrets are out there, fewer hidden gems that no one is aware of. But the ability to execute swiftly is a competitive advantage, as is a willingness to move into smaller markets. As that equity fund executive said, "We're not in the salty six," referring to the gateway markets of New York City; Boston; Washington, D.C.; Seattle; the Bay Area; and southern California.

The most likely behavior for the private equity fund in the next couple of years is heightened activity, and greater deal velocity on the sell side. Alpha investors make money by booking profits and moving on. Between 2011 and 2012, while many other investor groups were reluctant to buy "on the come," private funds placed $202 billion into real property assets. Price recovery now makes those purchases look very smart.

A REIT CEO marvels, "Private equity has a ton of money. I would say the fastest-growing source of capital is private equity at the moment." A good track record is the best argument to

Exhibit 2-12 Global Real Estate Investment in the United States as a Percentage of Total Sales

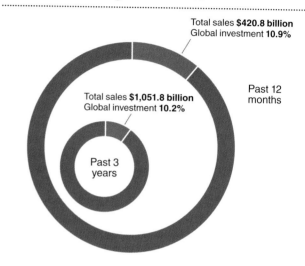

Total sales **$420.8 billion**
Global investment **10.9%**

Past 12 months

Total sales **$1,051.8 billion**
Global investment **10.2%**

Past 3 years

Source: Real Capital Analytics, as of June 2015.

offer when going out to raise fresh capital for deals in the years ahead.

International Investors

Where the money is coming from and how it is deployed can be characterized by a single word: "expanding." A Washington, D.C., private investor says, "Funds for real estate are growing every day, and international money is coming in droves." And,

Exhibit 2-11 Global Investment in U.S. Real Estate by Country

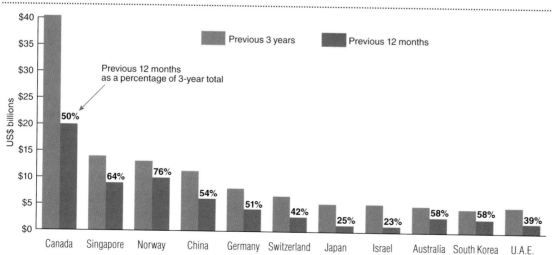

Previous 3 years   Previous 12 months

Previous 12 months as a percentage of 3-year total

Source: Real Capital Analytics, as of June 2015.

Exhibit 2-13 **Global Investment in U.S. Office Sector, by Five Largest Country Sources**

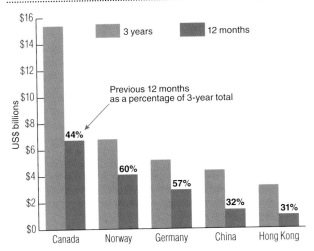

Source: Real Capital Analytics, as of July 31, 2014.

Exhibit 2-15 **Global Investment in U.S. Multifamily Sector, by Five Largest Country Sources**

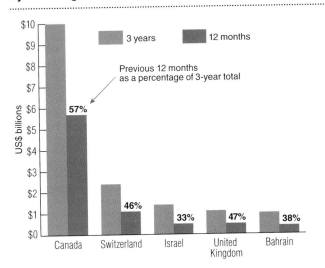

Source: Real Capital Analytics, as of June 2015.

Exhibit 2-14 **Global Investment in U.S. Retail Sector, by Five Largest Country Sources**

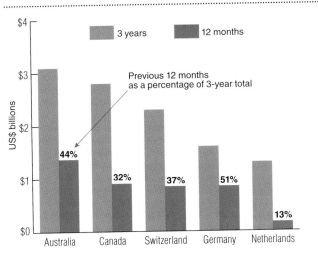

Source: Real Capital Analytics, as of June 2015.

Exhibit 2-16 **Global Investment in U.S. Industrial Sector, by Five Largest Country Sources**

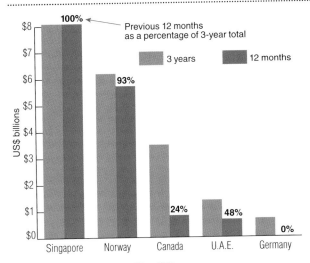

Source: Real Capital Analytics, as of June 2015.

yes, the gateway markets are still high on the list of top markets in the Association of Foreign Investors in Real Estate (AFIRE) annual survey. But, as an investment manager who had just returned from Singapore told us, **"World capital cannot be contained by the limited opportunities in just six coastal markets."** A fresh eye and open-mindedness are key attributes in putting that money to work in 2016.

A small firm that has been intermediating offshore real estate capital for a quarter-century said this in its *Emerging Trends* interview: "Our investors don't like the pricing in the gateways. We've made investments—value-add and opportunistic—in Orlando, St. Louis, and other markets, often in the suburbs where the flood of capital hasn't arrived yet." This firm invests international equity alongside some of the largest U.S. institu-

Exhibit 2-17 Global Investment in U.S. Hotel Sector, by Five Largest Country Sources

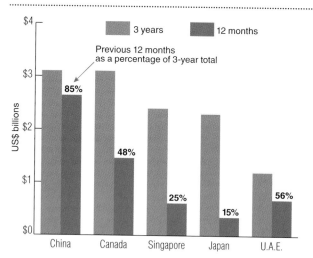

Source: Real Capital Analytics, as of June 2015.

tional investors, bringing deals to the value-add programs of the institutions. They report that the Middle East investors in particular "get it." Those investors are capital gains oriented and are quite willing to fund ground-up development in markets they believe will support it.

A top executive for a regional firm in the Southeast remarks about how offshore investors have discovered real estate in that area, following investments in manufacturing activities over the past several decades. He reports capital coming into the region from Germany, Italy, Japan, China, and Canada. "Everybody wants to be here," he says, and cites a much more welcoming environment and population diversity as contributing factors. Even last spring's uproar over the Confederate flag may have helped, as the ultimate decision on the part of South Carolina came down on the side of progress. "It's about damn time," in the view of this businessman.

Notwithstanding the geographic spread of offshore investment, the "salty six" still get the lion's share of inbound capital flows. From New York to Los Angeles, as well as in other coastal markets from Seattle to Miami, international investors know and covet U.S. cities with air and sea ports. This can be for development or for operating properties, by large institutions such as sovereign wealth funds and insurance companies or individuals (including EB-5 immigrants). When it is all summed up, net cross-border real estate investment amounted to a robust $31.2 billion for the 12 months ending June 2015. Given the continued uncertainties in Europe and the increasing volatility in Asia,

ample reason exists to see even more powerful capital flows into U.S. real estate markets in the coming period.

Crowdfunding

Watchful waiting continues to be the dominant perspective on crowdfunding by most of the *Emerging Trends* interviewees commenting on the topic. As discussed in chapter 1, it has recognized potential but carries risks that make many nervous. A model of capital raising still in its infancy (though with some historical precedents), crowdfunding may show impressive growth when measured on a percentage basis. But it is dwarfed by the other capital aggregates and is unlikely to scale to the point where it represents a meaningful competitor to the more traditional funding sources.

An investor/owner of office properties weighed in, saying, "I don't think [crowdfunding] is a good thing. Real estate is an industry where investors feel way more comfortable than they should [based on small-scale personal experience]: 'I've owned a house; I can own real estate.' And they make bad decisions." This is the same kind of fallacy of composition that equates household budgets to national budgets. Scale matters a great deal.

A banker is keeping an open mind for now: "I've met with a couple of the companies that are doing it. I think it has phenomenal potential. The challenge is making sure the companies that are doing it really add value. If it's wrapped in real hands-on assistance, where they can really help you get the books together and get everything in the right format, good. But if it's kind of a do-it-yourself, I'm not sure."

A pension fund manager, thinking in a broader perspective, sees crowdfunding as one of the pressures threatening the real estate brokerage industry. **"The important trend question is what sort of economic impact, in the long term, will social media and internet-based platforms, which include crowdfunding, have on commercial real estate? I think they'll disintermediate it.** Information about specific submarkets and deal sourcing will be dispersed along a lot more quickly." Again, it comes down to scale. Will there be a crowdfunding Zillow? And will large-scale investors be inclined to access such a source for deal making, more than just information gathering?

A firm in the capital-raising business asks, "Who are the sponsors? Crowdfunding is attempting to buy into the dot-com culture and there is a slight disconnect. I think there will be a lot of entries and failures. Crowdfunding is a mile wide, but only an inch deep. There is a lack of credibility: no background checks, no scrubbing, no due diligence."

We will be hearing more about crowdfunding as time goes on, especially during that period in which real estate as a whole is on the ascent. In the vernacular of social media, it will be "trending." The question on most people's minds is: "What happens when the cycle turns?"

Summing It Up

For 2016, and likely for some time thereafter, the background music for the *Emerging Trends* capital markets interviews was "You've Got to Accentuate the Positive." Without ignoring risk, the spirit of the industry right now is fairly upbeat. Some further duration to the upcycle is expected, and it is the rare person seeing any immediate recession for the economy or for the industry. Many indeed are inclined to think that we may have a "long top" to this recovery.

There are those with greater concerns, and they are taking some defensive moves by shortening investment horizons, shifting toward the income component of total return instead of expecting appreciation, and moving down the leverage scale to conserve capital. Undoubtedly, such a prudent approach will prove wise eventually, but will it leave money on the table (yes) and for how long?

For the latter years of this decade, it seems safe to say that the amassing of capital oriented to real estate will continue, but at a lesser pace than it has been from 2012 to 2015. The era ahead will be all about finding the best way to occupy the individual niche in a way that preserves capital and nourishes it in a way that promotes sustainable investment growth.

Markets to Watch

"2016 is the year of the secondary and tertiary markets. They continue to be more attractive on a relative opportunity basis than some of the gateway cities. Gateway cities, we know, are places people want to be, but we are thinking of cities like Nashville, Charlotte, Indianapolis, Louisville, Portland, Austin, Raleigh, Durham. These cities continue to attract lots of people. There are a lot of places that people love to live and work; they are manageable environments and have a better value proposition."

As the results of the *Emerging Trends in Real Estate 2016* survey were tabulated, it became evident that this was going to be a year of movement. Markets moved up and down in the rankings. A new market moved into the top position, while last year's number one fell to number 30. Markets entered the top ten and 20 spots for the first time while markets traditionally in the top five or ten slipped to lower positions. This result provoked the following question: Did it all make any sense?

Emerging Trends in Real Estate is a combination of an in-depth online survey and face-to-face interviews for a reason: It gives readers a more complete and well-rounded perspective of what market participants are thinking, or, to put it another way, a method to the madness.

Through the iterative process of reconciling survey results with interview notes, it became clear that markets were moving in the rankings as a result of market participants' feeling either the need to take a more offensive approach to the market, or to set up a desirable defensive position.

As the market senses an opportunity to play offense, participants are favoring cities with better growth opportunities—not a bad strategy in an environment where the economy is adding jobs and new supply is still tame by historical standards. These opportunities represent a combination of traditional higher-growth markets that offer favorable business conditions, markets that were slowed by the global financial crisis but are in a posi-

tion where demographics may drive future growth, and new markets that appear to be in a position to move up a class in the investment strata.

Another perspective on this market is to play some solid defense. The traditional "big six" markets have offered investors some perception of relative security since the days of the Great Recession. These markets, however, have become so highly valued on a global perspective that pricing has risen to levels that could make them slightly less attractive to a typical domestic investor. This position is not how everyone views these markets. A number of interviewees offered very logical positions for why they like the relative security of these top markets, and also where they see room for upside.

The result is whether one decides to play offense or defense, this real estate cycle is giving everyone a wide array of choices in a number of markets. It all comes down to calling the proper play and executing it to perfection.

2016 Market Rankings

In this year of movement, the *Emerging Trends in Real Estate* markets-to-watch survey reveals a new number-one market as Dallas/Fort Worth climbed four spots from last year's survey to take the top spot, leapfrogging state rival Austin in the process, which remains in the number-two spot. Nashville, Atlanta, and Portland, Oregon, are new entrants into the top ten for 2016, while Minneapolis and San Antonio enter the top 20. Economic

Exhibit 3-1 U.S. Markets to Watch: Overall Real Estate Prospects

	Investment	Development	Homebuilding		Investment	Development	Homebuilding
1 Dallas/Fort Worth (2, 3, 1)	3.87	3.79	4.34	39 Kansas City (42, 22, 38)	3.29	3.33	3.28
2 Austin (4, 1, 2)	3.82	3.83	4.17	40 Orlando (29, 34, 39)	3.41	3.20	3.27
3 Charlotte (11, 5, 4)	3.71	3.69	4.07	41 Fort Lauderdale (46, 52, 20)	3.26	2.99	3.57
4 Seattle (3, 10, 5)	3.84	3.57	4.00	42 Salt Lake City (45, 21, 45)	3.27	3.34	3.20
5 Atlanta (5, 6, 8)	3.79	3.68	3.93	43 Pittsburgh (35, 32, 48)	3.34	3.21	3.18
6 Denver (8, 13, 3)	3.74	3.51	4.14	44 Palm Beach (51, 49, 30)	3.20	3.03	3.42
7 Nashville (7, 2, 14)	3.75	3.81	3.67	45 Cincinnati (30, 36, 59)	3.40	3.20	2.99
8 San Francisco (9, 14, 12)	3.73	3.51	3.77	46 Cape Coral/Fort Myers/Naples (54,42,44)	3.15	3.10	3.23
9 Portland, OR (10, 7, 16)	3.71	3.63	3.64	47 New York–other boroughs (49, 46, 53)	3.23	3.07	3.15
10 Los Angeles (1, 8, 25)	3.87	3.61	3.50	48 Madison (39, 31, 66)	3.31	3.22	2.89
11 Raleigh/Durham (20, 15, 10)	3.57	3.50	3.88	49 Albuquerque (61, 37, 50)	3.04	3.19	3.17
12 San Jose (6, 11, 17)	3.78	3.54	3.61	50 Louisville (65, 55, 33)	3.01	2.98	3.40
13 Boston (14, 4, 27)	3.66	3.69	3.48	51 Washington, DC–MD suburbs (62,56,36)	3.04	2.97	3.36
14 Orange County (12, 26, 11)	3.68	3.31	3.78	52 New Orleans (59, 48, 47)	3.12	3.05	3.19
15 New York–Manhattan (13, 9, 40)	3.67	3.59	3.26	53 Jacksonville (63, 66, 26)	3.03	2.77	3.48
16 San Diego (16, 27, 19)	3.62	3.27	3.57	54 Boise (52, 60, 51)	3.19	2.90	3.16
17 Phoenix (17, 38, 15)	3.61	3.19	3.66	55 Des Moines (44, 43, 65)	3.27	3.09	2.89
18 Minneapolis/St. Paul (19, 16, 37)	3.59	3.48	3.28	56 Columbia (47, 63, 52)	3.24	2.84	3.15
19 Miami (25, 25, 22)	3.48	3.31	3.54	57 Cleveland (27, 40, 70)	3.42	3.14	2.64
20 San Antonio (36, 47, 7)	3.34	3.05	3.94	58 Westchester, NY/Fairfield, CT (57, 67, 54)	3.13	2.76	3.14
21 New York–Brooklyn (21, 12, 41)	3.54	3.51	3.25	59 Tacoma (26, 74, 57)	3.44	2.49	3.09
22 Indianapolis (18, 17, 42)	3.60	3.45	3.25	60 Oklahoma City (58, 61, 60)	3.13	2.87	2.98
23 Honolulu (40, 50, 9)	3.30	3.02	3.88	61 Sacramento (56, 58, 63)	3.14	2.91	2.91
24 Washington, DC–District (28, 39, 18)	3.42	3.19	3.59	62 Las Vegas (68, 53, 62)	2.99	2.98	2.95
25 Charleston (38, 18, 29)	3.32	3.40	3.44	63 Memphis (71, 70, 34)	2.82	2.66	3.40
26 Chicago (15, 24, 46)	3.64	3.32	3.20	64 Hartford (64, 65, 58)	3.01	2.79	3.00
27 Columbus (31, 20, 31)	3.38	3.34	3.41	65 Omaha (66, 57, 67)	3.00	2.94	2.83
28 Oakland/East Bay (32, 28, 24)	3.37	3.25	3.51	66 Richmond (67, 64, 64)	3.00	2.81	2.89
29 Tampa/St. Petersburg (33, 35, 23)	3.36	3.20	3.54	67 Birmingham (69, 69, 61)	2.95	2.69	2.96
30 Houston (50, 59, 6)	3.23	2.91	3.96	68 Milwaukee (60, 54, 72)	3.05	2.98	2.55
31 Philadelphia (34, 29, 32)	3.35	3.22	3.41	69 Virginia Beach/Norfolk (72, 72, 56)	2.74	2.65	3.11
32 Washington, DC–Northern VA (24,41,35)	3.51	3.11	3.36	70 Tucson (48, 73, 75)	3.24	2.56	2.50
33 Detroit (23, 23, 55)	3.51	3.33	3.12	71 Providence (70, 68, 71)	2.92	2.75	2.61
34 St. Louis (41, 33, 28)	3.29	3.21	3.44	72 Spokane (53, 75, 68)	3.19	2.17	2.81
35 Baltimore (37, 19, 43)	3.33	3.37	3.23	73 Portland, ME (73, 62, 73)	2.66	2.87	2.55
36 Inland Empire (43, 45, 21)	3.28	3.08	3.56	74 Buffalo (75, 51, 74)	2.49	2.99	2.53
37 Northern New Jersey (22, 30, 49)	3.52	3.22	3.17	75 Deltona/Daytona (74, 71, 69)	2.55	2.66	2.66
38 Greenville (55, 44, 13)	3.14	3.08	3.68				

Source: *Emerging Trends in Real Estate 2016* survey.

Note: Numbers in parentheses are rankings for, in order, investment, development, and homebuilding.

growth potential seems to be the reason behind the movement of markets within and into the top 20 for 2016. The market may be poised to take a more offensive approach in 2016 as the economy strengthens and real estate fundamentals improve.

The movement was not all in a positive direction, however. Houston provided the most dramatic move, falling from number one to number 30. Concern over what the fall in the price of oil combined with the current level of new development gave survey respondents pause for 2016. San Francisco, a perennial top market, slipped from number three to number eight. Other big-six markets slipping in the top 20 include Los Angeles, Boston, and the Manhattan submarket of New York City. Chicago slipped slightly, dropping just out of the top 20 and ending up at number 26.

The consensus for the movement of these markets seems to be related to their current pricing rather than their relative attractiveness as markets. A number of interviewees and survey respondents feel that these are still excellent defensive investment markets. The final big-six market—Washington, D.C.—slipped again this year to number 24. Survey respondents remain cautious about the economic condition of the market and the amount of new supply still being delivered.

Notable moves outside the top 20 include Tampa Bay/St. Petersburg and Columbus, Ohio, which moved into the top 30.

Orlando, Fort Lauderdale, and the metropolitan statistical areas (MSAs) making up southwest Florida also joined Tampa as Florida markets improving in this year's survey.

Market Trends

What could lead to the market movement in the *Emerging Trends in Real Estate 2016* survey? The following five trends were identified by interviewees as potentially leading to the changes in survey respondents' outlook for each market. These trends are seen as having positive and negative influences on a number of cities in the survey.

Look Out for the "Villes" . . . and Pittsburgh

Survey respondents and interviewees both expressed an interest in the "villes," loosely defined as markets such as Nashville and Knoxville, Tennessee, and Jacksonville and Gainesville, Florida. The sentiment, however, is not limited to the similarity in the names. The real meaning behind this trend relates to what is going on in these markets and others with similar economic, demographic, and cultural characteristics.

The "villes" are seen as offering opportunities to take advantage of faster-growing demographics, economies, concentrations in desirable industries, and, in many cases, aggressive development plans to establish growth centers within the community. A number of these markets appear to offer benefits similar to key 18-hour cities: growing urban centers, good in-migration (specifically among desired workers), attractive quality of life, and a lower cost of doing business.

Nashville is a market that has been mentioned numerous times in interviews over the past three years, and this year survey respondents have moved the market up significantly in terms of perceived attractiveness. What market may be on the horizon as the future Nashville? How about Pittsburgh? Pittsburgh has seen fairly stable survey results, but the number of mentions during interviews is trending up. Interviewees cite the growth in science, technology, engineering, and math (STEM) employment and a strong education and medical sector as creating investment opportunities in the market.

Florida's Resurgence Continues

In last year's survey, Miami made it back into the top 20. This year, the entire state of Florida is being viewed in a very positive light. Along with the primary southeast Florida markets, survey respondents and interviewees like the rest of the state as well. The position of Orlando and Tampa both improved noticeably in this year's survey. Other markets such as southwest Florida and Jacksonville continued to improve.

The Florida markets are benefiting from the country finally returning to normal levels of mobility after the temporary freeze created by the housing market collapse. The result has been improved levels of population and employment growth. One interviewee noted, "The real tailwind to Florida growth created by retiring baby boomers is still to come." While markets in Florida have similar characteristics, they offer diversity in the form of economic opportunities. The different regions and markets appear poised to benefit from an improving U.S. economy.

Respondents Get Cautious about High-Priced Markets

Survey respondents and interviewees both really like the big-six markets, but this is how a number of interviewees would characterize their views of the markets: While they do not disagree that the investment performance in markets such as New York and San Francisco has been phenomenal, the question is whether it is too late to invest in these markets now. One interviewee put it this way: "If I was going to invest in San Francisco with pricing where it is now, I would have to be planning on holding the asset for at least ten years." Coincidentally, this appears to be the strategy for a significant amount of foreign capital coming into these markets. This has prompted a number of interviewees to raise the following question: "What will these markets look like with a number of trophy assets off the market for possibly 25 years or longer?"

Survey respondents appear to echo the questions raised by the interviewees. A number of the big-six markets have slipped in the 2016 rankings. The markets are still seen as attractive, just maybe priced at a level that requires some extra diligence. *Emerging Trends in Real Estate 2014* presented how survey respondents preferred the big six to the field; 2016 could well be the year when the field closes the gap.

Growth and Affordability Drive Market Sentiment

"My investment recommendation is to identify a growth path and put yourself right in front of it." That was the specific advice from one interviewee, but it is a sentiment voiced by many more. As the market begins to express some reticence about the market possibilities available in the big six, what other markets do they see as offering opportunities? The answer is as diverse as the real estate market itself, but finding markets that are showing signs of significant growth tops the list for almost everyone.

The dominance of "growth" markets in this year's top ten is a testament to current market sentiment. Survey respondents and interviewees like markets such as Dallas/Fort Worth and Atlanta, citing that the current growth pattern along with restrained levels of new construction makes this a good time to invest in these markets. Another factor that is prevalent among the top markets for 2016 is the affordability and ease of doing business. Dallas/Fort Worth, Atlanta, Nashville, and Portland are all seeing company relocations to augment organic employment growth.

Housing Outlook Continues to Improve

A driving component behind the improved outlook for a number of markets is the housing market. Last year, we commented that housing was ready to step off the roller coaster. It appears that in a majority of markets, housing has indeed stabilized and is poised to begin a sustained upward trajectory. Another 2015 trend was that peak levels of millennials and baby boomers would be making housing decisions in the next five years. This could have a significantly positive impact on housing: millennials buying their first homes and baby boomers either downsizing or retiring to a new home or perhaps purchasing a second home.

The locales that will benefit the most from the movement of these two generational titans are still subject to a certain amount of speculation, but one thing is certain: most markets will need to add housing to keep up with any type of increase in demand. The increase in housing stock, both single-family and multifamily, has lagged household growth in many markets. When one factors in that the number of home purchases is quickly getting back to average historical levels, it becomes apparent that more

housing stock will be needed. It will be interesting to watch the market determine what that housing stock will look like.

Fall in Oil Prices Affects Energy-Dependent Markets

Last year's interviews and surveys were conducted with oil prices climbing steadily toward $100 a barrel, so it was no surprise when Houston—which had been in the top ten in previous years—moved to the number-one spot. What a difference a year can make! As oil prices have plummeted into the $40-per-barrel range, survey respondents are not confident in Houston real estate for the coming year. Houston drops to number 30 in this year's survey, a drop that exceeds that of Washington, D.C., which fell out of the top 20 in the 2014 survey. Healthy debate is good, and there are some differences of opinion on the outlook for Houston. One interviewee summed it up thusly: "The Houston situation would make a great science experiment. We will get to see if all of the economic diversification that has taken place over the past 20 to 30 years can help offset an oil price shock." Other interviewees see the perceived weakness in the Houston market as potentially a buying opportunity in what they feel is still a vibrant market. The bottom line: Houston may be in for an interesting couple of years, with detractors and cheerleaders debating its future.

The Top 20 Markets

Dallas/Fort Worth (1). Impressive employment growth is the story behind the Dallas/Fort Worth metropolitan area's rise to the top of this year's survey. Multiple survey respondents and interviewees mentioned the strong job growth driving the local economy. This job growth is supported by a business-friendly environment along with an attractive cost of doing business and cost of living that has allowed the Dallas/Fort Worth market to enjoy the benefits of corporate relocations.

Survey respondents were positive regarding all property types in the Dallas/Fort Worth market and in both the investment and development potential. Concerns about potential overbuilding are on the market's mind, but the sentiment is that new construction is still justified at this time. The outlook for the single-family

market remains very strong in Dallas/Fort Worth. The view of market participants in the Dallas/Fort Worth market is the highest in the South region and one of the strongest in the nation. The market continues to benefit from strong investor

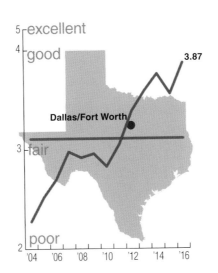

interest, plenty of available capital, and a strong local development community.

Austin (2). One of the inaugural 18-hour cities, the Texas state capital has become a perennial favorite among survey respondents. This optimism has been rewarded by continued strong economic and real estate performance. Austin continues to benefit from diverse job creation ranging from service jobs to higher-end STEM and technology, advertising, media, and information (TAMI) positions. Austin remains an attractive place to live for all generations. If there is a concern about Austin, it may be that the market is growing faster than the local infrastructure.

The 2016 outlook for all property types in Austin is well above average, but survey respondents were particularly favorable toward single-family and retail. Austin may well be a market where the growth in population leads to the need for new

Exhibit 3-2 **U.S. Office Property Buy/Hold/Sell Recommendations**

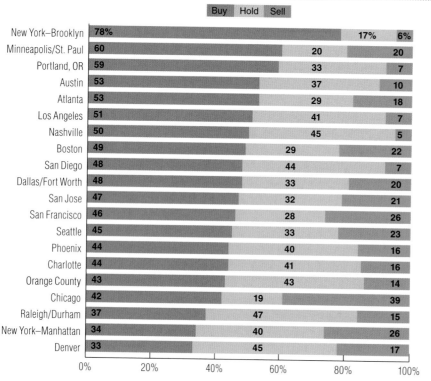

	Buy	Hold	Sell
New York–Brooklyn	78%	17%	6%
Minneapolis/St. Paul	60	20	20
Portland, OR	59	33	7
Austin	53	37	10
Atlanta	53	29	18
Los Angeles	51	41	7
Nashville	50	45	5
Boston	49	29	22
San Diego	48	44	7
Dallas/Fort Worth	48	33	20
San Jose	47	32	21
San Francisco	46	28	26
Seattle	45	33	23
Phoenix	44	40	16
Charlotte	44	41	16
Orange County	43	43	14
Chicago	42	19	39
Raleigh/Durham	37	47	15
New York–Manhattan	34	40	26
Denver	33	45	17

Source: *Emerging Trends in Real Estate 2016* survey.

Note: Cities listed are the top 20 rated for investment in the office sector; cities are listed in order of the relative percentage of "buy" recommendations.

retail centers. The perception of the local real estate market by Austin respondents remains very good, with all categories in the good-to-excellent range. The only

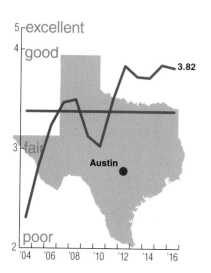

potential shortcoming perceived by the local market is in public and private investment.

Charlotte (3). The largest city in North Carolina continues to embody many of the components of an 18-hour city that the *Emerging Trends in Real Estate 2015* report introduced. Good job and population growth along with the development of urban centers continues to make the market attractive to residents. Interviewees generally feel good about the Charlotte market, although some did express concern that the concentration of the financial services industry may not offer the same level of growth as other more technology-oriented markets.

Housing is the sector that has the strongest 2016 outlook in the Charlotte market.

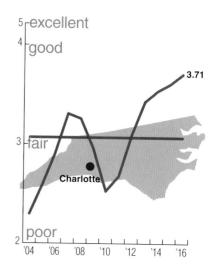

This is similar to many of the faster-growing affordable markets in the survey. Industrial, to serve the growing local economy, and hotels, to handle growing numbers of business and leisure travelers, are the two highest-rated commercial sectors. The local view of the Charlotte market is very strong, with the only sector not scoring in the good-to-excellent range being development opportunities.

Seattle (4). The Seattle market has become so popular with domestic and global investors that in interviews it is not unusual for it to be added to the list of top six markets. Clearly, 2016 survey respondents feel the same way. Seattle has a diverse industry base and is benefiting from growth in the TAMI industries. One interviewee noted that Seattle is one of those markets where the growth has been strong enough, long enough, that the only potential risk is being able to sustain its current pace.

The 2016 outlook for all the commercial sectors of the Seattle market is relatively strong with the exception of hotels. The outlook for hotels is good, just not as good as that for the rest of the market. A growing population base and legitimate constraints on supply make the single-family housing market the most attractive

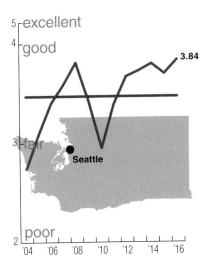

sector for 2016. The local outlook for the economy and investor demand could not be much stronger in Seattle. In fact, a lack of development opportunities and public and private investment is seen as the only potential problem from a local market perspective.

Atlanta (5). Interviewees and survey respondents agree that the Georgia state capital is solidly in a sweet spot with regard to growth and new supply. The market is enjoying strong growth in key sectors of the economy without the typical concerns about oversupply. The lower cost of doing business is attracting corporate relocations that are contribut-

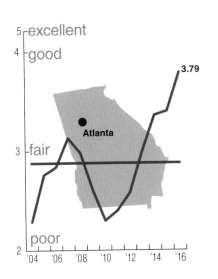

Exhibit 3-3 U.S. Retail Property Buy/Hold/Sell Recommendations

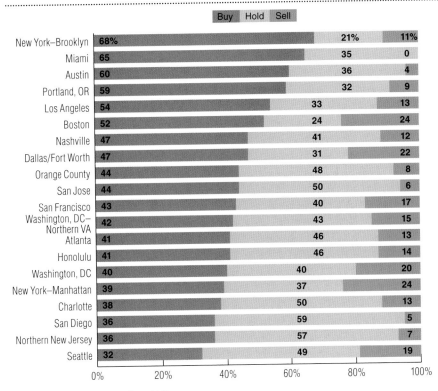

	Buy	Hold	Sell
New York–Brooklyn	68%	21%	11%
Miami	65	35	0
Austin	60	36	4
Portland, OR	59	32	9
Los Angeles	54	33	13
Boston	52	24	24
Nashville	47	41	12
Dallas/Fort Worth	47	31	22
Orange County	44	48	8
San Jose	44	50	6
San Francisco	43	40	17
Washington, DC–Northern VA	42	43	15
Atlanta	41	46	13
Honolulu	41	46	14
Washington, DC	40	40	20
New York–Manhattan	39	37	24
Charlotte	38	50	13
San Diego	36	59	5
Northern New Jersey	36	57	7
Seattle	32	49	19

Source: *Emerging Trends in Real Estate 2016* survey.

Note: Cities listed are the top 20 rated for investment in the retail sector; cities are listed in order of the relative percentage of "buy" recommendations.

ing to market growth. As one interviewee remarked, "If you get into this market now, you will be ahead of the curve when new development gets fully underway."

Survey respondents have a favorable view of all sectors of the Atlanta real estate market, with no particular sector standing out significantly from the others. The local outlook for the Atlanta market is good, led by relatively strong outlooks for the local economy, investor demand, and capital availability. The weakest component of the local market is the perceived accomplishments of public and private investment.

Denver (6). The strength of the economy in Colorado's state capital seems to have put it on everyone's list of top markets for 2016. Survey respondents and interview-

ees both commented on the favorable outlook for the market. Denver has taken advantage of a location and a culture that are attractive to a qualified workforce

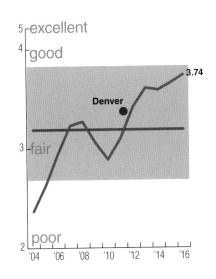

and exposure to growing technology industries. In addition, a number of public and private infrastructure investments are setting the stage for future sustainable growth.

The single-family housing market is expected to remain hot in 2016. Survey respondents picked single-family housing to have the best outlook for next year. The industrial market also is projected to offer good investment opportunities in the coming year. Local Denver market participants are understandably optimistic about 2016. The overall outlook of good to excellent is led by a strong perception of investor demand, the strength of the local economy, and capital availability. While it is the lowest-scored component, public and private investment is still one of the highest scores in the survey.

Nashville (7). Tennessee's state capital has been on the lips of interviewees the last two years as a potential up-and-coming market. Well, it looks like it has up and come. Survey respondents have caught up with the interviewees and Nashville is a top-ten market for 2016. Nashville is another market that embodies the 18-hour city amenities that include a growing and vibrant urban core, but that also offers attractive suburban locations. Similar to Austin, the only noticeable

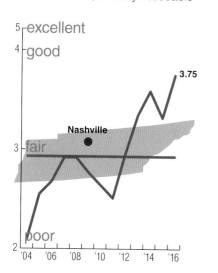

concern from interviewees is whether the current infrastructure will be able to keep up with growth at its current pace.

Office is the property type that survey respondents anticipate will offer the best investment opportunity in 2016. According to local market participants, the Nashville economy should be firing on all cylinders in 2016. Local respondents see an extremely strong local economy supported by plenty of investor demand and available capital—all factors that a strong local development community can put to good use.

San Francisco (8). The San Francisco market is back to peak levels in just about every market component: occupancy, rent levels, and valuations. This may be why survey responders and interview-

ees alike are taking a more conservative approach to the market. One interviewee noted: "The good thing about San Francisco is that even if it does drop, the chances are it will bounce back even

Exhibit 3-4 U.S. Hotel Property Buy/Hold/Sell Recommendations

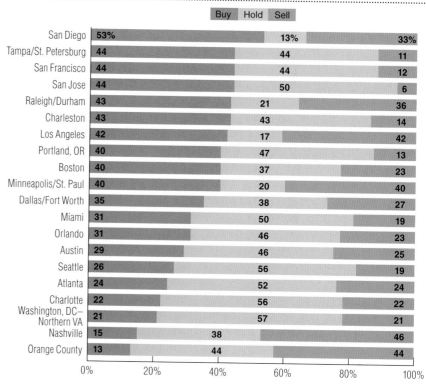

	Buy	Hold	Sell
San Diego	53%	13%	33%
Tampa/St. Petersburg	44	44	11
San Francisco	44	44	12
San Jose	44	50	6
Raleigh/Durham	43	21	36
Charleston	43	43	14
Los Angeles	42	17	42
Portland, OR	40	47	13
Boston	40	37	23
Minneapolis/St. Paul	40	20	40
Dallas/Fort Worth	35	38	27
Miami	31	50	19
Orlando	31	46	23
Austin	29	46	25
Seattle	26	56	19
Atlanta	24	52	24
Charlotte	22	56	22
Washington, DC–Northern VA	21	57	21
Nashville	15	38	46
Orange County	13	44	44

Source: *Emerging Trends in Real Estate 2016* survey.

Note: Cities listed are the top 20 rated for investment in the hotel sector; cities are listed in order of the relative percentage of "buy" recommendations.

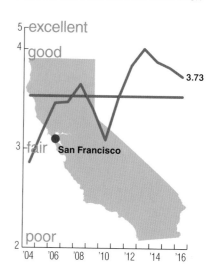

higher." That may explain why even with a market back at peak levels, survey respondents still feel like it belongs in the top ten.

Every real estate sector in San Francisco could arguably be called hot, but survey respondents like the outlook for hotel and single-family residential for 2016. The rest of the national market may have some reservations about the San Francisco market, but that does not seem to apply to the local market. The local outlook score for San Francisco is the highest in the survey—a score that is even more impressive when one considers that the outlook for development opportunities is only fair.

Portland, Oregon (9). Along with a few other select markets, Portland may arguably have been at the forefront of the attributes that make up the core of what constitutes an 18-hour city. As such, it is definitely a market that interviewees like to hold up as an example of what they like to see in market characteristics. That being said, there is still some hesitation among all national investors to embrace Portland as a true primary market. It will be interesting to see whether 2016 is the beginning of Portland's rise from top secondary market to primary market.

The 2016 outlook for investment by Portland property type is led by the industrial and office sectors. The two commercial property types are higher than both of the residential-related sectors. Portland survey respondents feel good about their local market, but do see some room for improvement in public and private investment and the local development community.

Los Angeles (10). As the largest big-six market on the West Coast, Los Angeles continues to be a favorite among interviewees and survey respondents. Pricing and fundamentals are strong, but are relatively mild compared with those in San Francisco. Interviewees remarked on the potential for future growth in select Los Angeles neighborhoods.

Two property sectors typically viewed as undersupplied in Los Angeles have the highest outlook score in this year's survey. Multifamily has the highest score, followed closely by retail. In some respects, the Los Angeles local outlook matches the national opinion of the market—good and steady. While the outlook for the local economy is just good, investor demand and capital availability are stronger, matching more closely what interviewees and all survey respondents seem to think about Los Angeles.

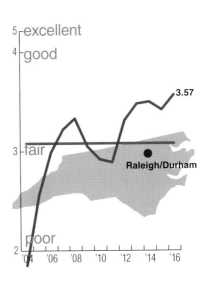

Raleigh/Durham (11). The Raleigh/Durham metro area built on its strong position in last year's survey and has been added to a large number of top market lists. The concentration of educational facilities along with a growing technology sector is driving the economy, and the development of attractive urban centers is making the cities within the Raleigh/Durham area appealing as places to live. Interviewees are drawn to the growth in the STEM industries and the potential this adds to longer-term growth.

The single-family residential market was selected by survey respondents to have the best outlook for 2016. This is likely driven by the expectations for strong household growth in the market. The local Raleigh/Durham market is optimistic about 2016: The overall local outlook is in the good-to-excellent range, driven by a very strong outlook for the local economy and investor demand.

San Jose (12). Technology is still seen as the driver of economic growth in the United States, and San Jose is still viewed as the center of that growth. A new facet of the conversation concerning San Jose is the urbanization of the technology industry to San Francisco. Several interviewees mentioned that it

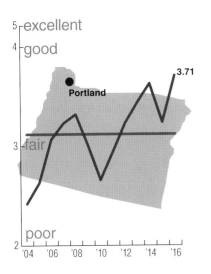

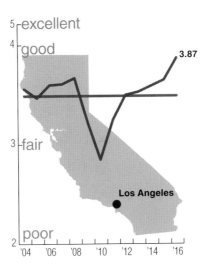

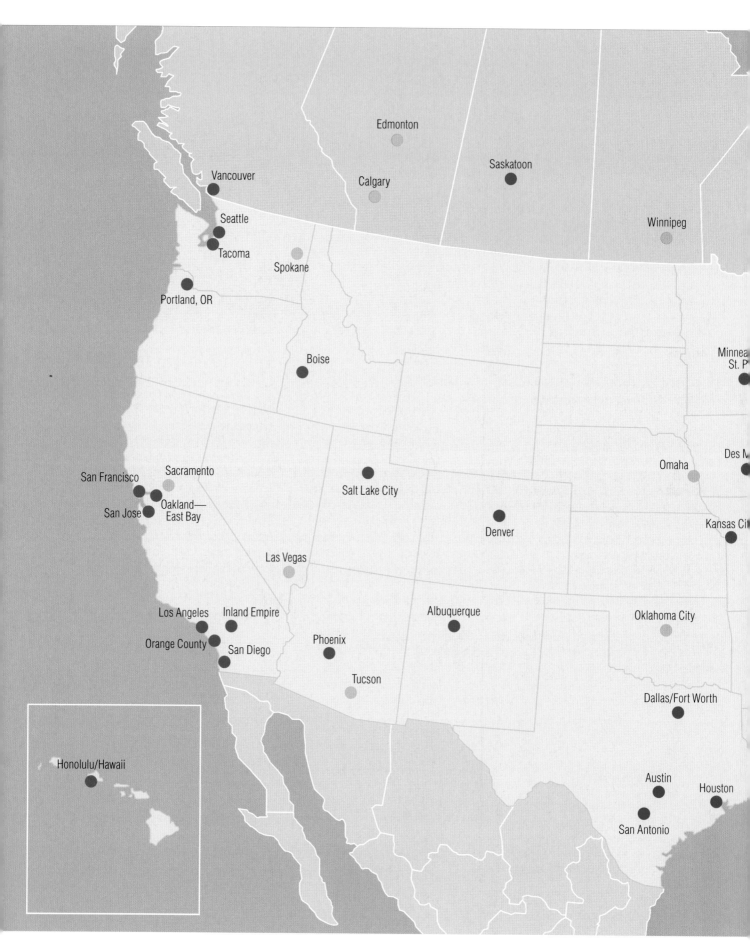

Edmonton

Saskatoon

Vancouver

Calgary

Winnipeg

Seattle

Tacoma

Spokane

Portland, OR

Boise

Minnea St. P

San Francisco

Sacramento

Des M

Omaha

Oakland—
East Bay

Salt Lake City

San Jose

Kansas Cit

Denver

Las Vegas

Los Angeles

Inland Empire

Albuquerque

Oklahoma City

Orange County

San Diego

Phoenix

Tucson

Dallas/Fort Worth

Honolulu/Hawaii

Austin

Houston

San Antonio

Halifax

Montreal

Ottawa

Portland, ME

Boston

Toronto

Providence

Buffalo

Hartford

Westchester, NY/Fairfield, CT

son

Milwaukee

Detroit

Northern New Jersey

New York—other boroughs

New York—Brooklyn

Chicago

Cleveland

Pittsburgh

New York—Manhattan

Indianapolis

Columbus

Washington, DC—
MD suburbs

Baltimore

Philadelphia

St. Louis

Cincinnati

Richmond

Washington, DC—District

Louisville

Washington, DC—Northern VA

Memphis

Nashville

Charlotte

Raleigh/Durham

Virginia Beach/Norfolk

Greenville

Atlanta

Columbia

Charleston

Birmingham

Jacksonville

New Orleans

Deltona/Daytona

Orlando

Tampa/
St. Petersburg

Palm Beach

Fort Lauderdale

Cape Coral/Fort Myers/Naples

Miami

Leading U.S./Canadian Cities

Overall Real Estate Prospects

● Generally good

● Fair

● Generally poor

Note: Numbers represent metro-area overall
country rank.

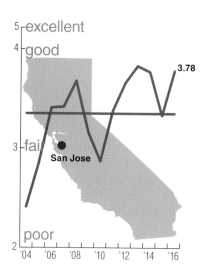

5 — excellent
4 — good
3.78
3 — fair
San Jose
2 — poor
'04 '06 '08 '10 '12 '14 '16

Exhibit 3-5 U.S. Multifamily Property Buy/Hold/Sell Recommendations

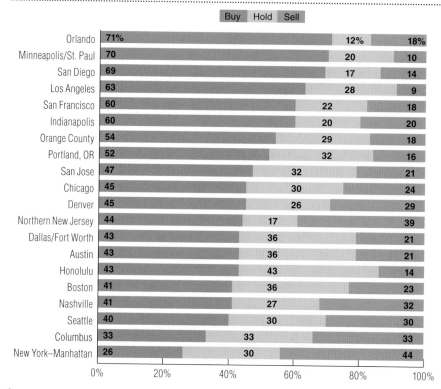

	Buy	Hold	Sell
Orlando	71%	12%	18%
Minneapolis/St. Paul	70	20	10
San Diego	69	17	14
Los Angeles	63	28	9
San Francisco	60	22	18
Indianapolis	60	20	20
Orange County	54	29	18
Portland, OR	52	32	16
San Jose	47	32	21
Chicago	45	30	24
Denver	45	26	29
Northern New Jersey	44	17	39
Dallas/Fort Worth	43	36	21
Austin	43	36	21
Honolulu	43	43	14
Boston	41	36	23
Nashville	41	27	32
Seattle	40	30	30
Columbus	33	33	33
New York–Manhattan	26	30	44

0%   20%   40%   60%   80%   100%

Source: *Emerging Trends in Real Estate 2016* survey.

Note: Cities listed are the top 20 rated for investment in the multifamily sector; cities are listed in order of the relative percentage of "buy" recommendations.

will be interesting to see how this could change the dynamic between the two Bay Area metro areas. One thing that interviewees did agree on is that San Jose is still the most desirable technology campus location.

As one of the highest-cost housing markets in the country, it is not surprising that San Jose multifamily housing and single-family housing were selected by the survey as the two property types with the best outlook for 2016. The local outlook among San Jose market participants is very good, but somewhat bifurcated. The local economy, investor demand, and capital availability all received very strong scores, while the other components were merely good.

Boston (13). It was a relatively quiet year for the Massachusetts state capital. Survey respondents still like the market, but it did slip out of the top ten this year. Interviewees remarked that Boston is becoming an increasingly neighborhood-driven market. It continues to be viewed as one of the top lab markets in the country, and good growth in STEM industries should support that position. Interviewees also like the continued concentration in education and medical employment in the market.

According to this year's survey, the Boston office sector had the highest outlook score of all Boston property sectors for 2016. Multifamily came in as the second-highest property type score and

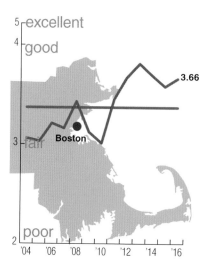

5 — excellent
4 — good
3.66
3 — fair
Boston
2 — poor
'04 '06 '08 '10 '12 '14 '16

the highest residential-related property type. Slipping out of the overall top ten has not diminished the local real estate community's confidence in the Boston market. The overall score is one of the top in the survey and is led by a strong outlook for investor demand and capital availability.

Orange County (14). Orange County appears to have fully rebounded from the collapse of the subprime mortgage industry that drove growth until the global financial crisis. The market is now more reliant on the traditional small businesses that make up a large percentage of the tenant base. A number of these firms are involved with foreign trade, so they continue to benefit from a growing local economy. One question posed by interviewees is the following: What impact

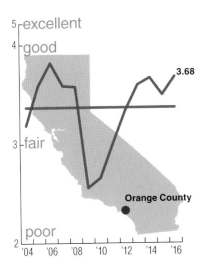

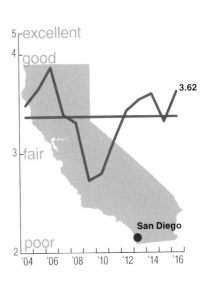

could a strong dollar have on this sector of the economy?

As in other higher-cost housing markets, the multifamily sector is the highest-scoring property type for Orange County in this year's survey. As in the other West Coast markets, the local Orange County respondents see strength in investor demand and capital availability. The outlook for the local economy in 2016 is also good, but the outlooks for the other local market components are scored relatively lower.

New York—Manhattan (15). Manhattan remains one of the top global markets for investment, but the competition from global capital may be hurting its position with survey respondents. Several interviewees remarked that the competition for assets is so intense that the market is out of reach for a number of investors. This may force investors to seek other areas for opportunities; it certainly does not diminish the health of the market for other segments who still view Manhattan as an attractive place in which to do business. If an area for concern exists, it is the cost of doing business there. With a number of new projects underway, will the market be able to afford to attract the quality of worker needed to keep the economy growing?

Retail is the highest-scoring sector for New York in the 2016 survey, with the multifamily sector a close second. Investor demand and capital availability are viewed by the local New York market as definite strengths for 2016. If there is a weakness in the market, it is in the availability of development opportunities and public/private investment cooperation.

San Diego (16). In this year's survey, San Diego moved up from number 20 in last year's survey. A number of interviewees have started adding San Diego to their list of markets that they see as having the potential to outperform in 2016. The typical reason given is the concentration in life sciences and technology. These industries are seen as having significant tailwinds because of the aging of the U.S. population.

Survey respondents feel the most optimism toward the residential real estate sector, with single-family and multifamily as the leading sectors for the market. The local market outlook for San Diego is one of the lowest for a top-20 market. Local respondents feel relatively good about the local economy, investor demand, and capital availability. The real weakness in the 2016 local outlook comes from public/

private investment and the availability of development opportunities.

Phoenix (17). Phoenix is back to being a high-growth market, having shaken off many of the ill-effects from the global financial crisis. Interviewees like the growth potential there, especially in sectors that will benefit from the growing population base. Some concern exists, however, that the potential for new development could be starting prematurely.

The 2016 outlook for the commercial and residential sectors in Phoenix are fairly even. The sectors that stand to benefit directly from stronger population growth

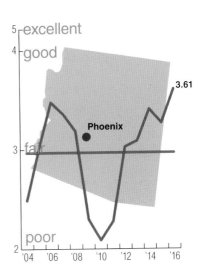

are ranked slightly higher than the other sectors. The industrial sector should benefit from an increase in regional and local distribution. The local Phoenix market may be slightly more conservative in its outlook than the broader survey group. The local perception of the economy and investor demand remain good, but capital availability and development opportunities are seen as being slightly weaker.

Minneapolis/St. Paul (18). Minneapolis/St. Paul is the highest-ranked midwestern market in this year's survey. Minneapolis is enjoying strong growth in the education and medical sectors along with being a regional center for STEM employment. A vibrant neighborhood culture is the reason cited most often by interviewees for being attracted to Minneapolis/St. Paul, making the region attractive to an educated workforce.

The commercial real estate sectors are seen as offering the best opportunities in 2016. Industrial has the highest score because the Minneapolis/St. Paul industrial market benefits from a stronger local and regional economy. Unlike many other markets in this year's survey, the single-family sector is actually one of the lower-rated components of the market. The local market outlook is perceived as relatively strong, although

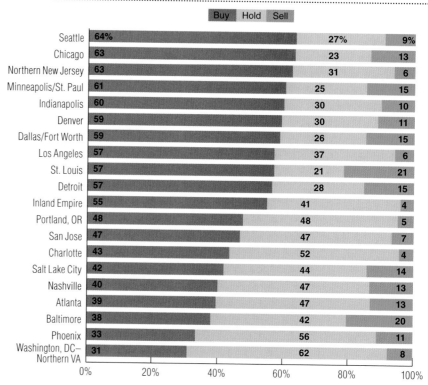

Exhibit 3-6 **U.S. Industrial Property Buy/Hold/Sell Recommendations**

	Buy	Hold	Sell
Seattle	64%	27%	9%
Chicago	63	23	13
Northern New Jersey	63	31	6
Minneapolis/St. Paul	61	25	15
Indianapolis	60	30	10
Denver	59	30	11
Dallas/Fort Worth	59	26	15
Los Angeles	57	37	6
St. Louis	57	21	21
Detroit	57	28	15
Inland Empire	55	41	4
Portland, OR	48	48	5
San Jose	47	47	7
Charlotte	43	52	4
Salt Lake City	42	44	14
Nashville	40	47	13
Atlanta	39	47	13
Baltimore	38	42	20
Phoenix	33	56	11
Washington, DC– Northern VA	31	62	8

Source: *Emerging Trends in Real Estate 2016* survey.

Note: Cities listed are the top 20 rated for investment in the industrial sector; cities are listed in order of the relative percentage of "buy" recommendations.

lower compared with the outlook for the rest of the top 20. While the local economy and investor demand are perceived as good, the local development community and public/private investment are seen as somewhat weaker than the rest of the market.

Miami (19). Miami remains in the top 20 this year, and the outlook from survey respondents and interviewees alike seems to be more optimistic. Interviewees cited the potential for continued growth in the Miami economy along with comparatively strong supply constraints as reasons for optimism.

The retail sector has the strongest outlook in the Miami market. Retail is seen as benefiting from good population and income growth as well as the strong tour-

ism component in the market. It remains to be seen if the strong dollar and an economic slowdown in Latin America will be a headwind to Miami's continued improvement. Local market participants

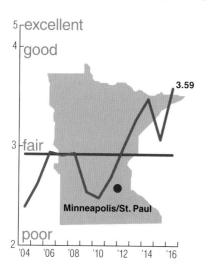

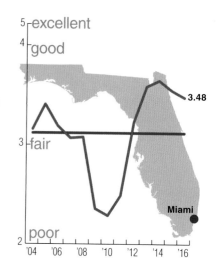

feel very good about the local economy in Miami and rate overall prospects as good to excellent. If an area of concern exists, it is one of success: the lowest-rated component of the local market is the availability of development opportunities.

San Antonio (20). San Antonio moves into the top 20 this year, but not without a few questions. The economy is exhibiting strong growth, but concerns exist about negative implications resulting from the fall in oil prices and any negative repercussions this could have on the local economy. On a positive note, a reduction in labor demand for the oil fields could provide a boost to the San Antonio labor

force that must compete for qualified workers.

The local housing market, both single-family and multifamily, is viewed as offering two of the best investment opportunities, with the other commercial sectors viewed as offering good potential for 2016. The local view is good for San Antonio, although survey respondents would like to see the opportunity for more public and private investment opportunities. Respondents in San Antonio, a secondary market, are not as confident in continued investor demand and capital availability as respondents in many of the primary markets.

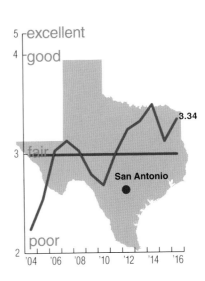

Perspectives on Regions

The outlook for U.S. regions for 2016 reflects the continued improvement in the outlook for more markets. The West and South regions both exhibit improved outlooks for all property types, and local market participants on average feel more positive about the current environment. The general positive feeling for 2016 continues the positive outlook reported for 2015. The Northeast and Midwest regional average results also are generally positive, with any decline in outlook from 2015 limited to a few property types.

West Region

The 20 markets that make up the West region have an average rank of 33 in this year's survey. This is the highest average rank of all four U.S. regions represented. The region includes four of the top ten markets and an impressive eight of the top 20.

Survey respondents like the multifamily sector as the highest-scoring property type in the region. Multifamily markets projected to easily outperform the regional average include San Jose, Orange County, Los Angeles, San Diego, and Honolulu.

After multifamily, survey respondents like industrial, single-family housing, retail, hotel, and office in the West region. Industrial markets expected to outperform the regional average include the following: Los Angeles, Denver, the Inland Empire, Salt Lake

Exhibit 3-7 Local Outlook: West Region

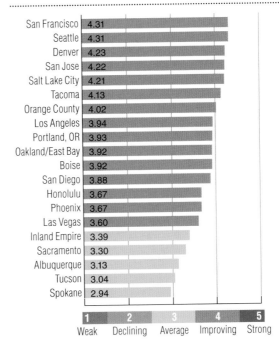

Source: *Emerging Trends in Real Estate 2016* survey.

Note: Average score of local market participants' opinions on strength of local economy, investor demand, capital availability, development and redevelopment opportunities, public/private investments, and local development community.

Exhibit 3-8 Economy

Market	2016 Population			Millennials (age 16–35)		Business costs					Total employment			Location quotient****				
	Total (millions)	2015–2016 % change	5-year annual net migration (000s)	% of total population	5-year growth	2016 GMP per capita ratio*	GMP per capita 5-year projected growth	Cost of doing business**	Per capita disposable income ratio***	5-year disposable income growth	2015–2016 % change	2016 as % of previous peak	2018 as % of previous peak	Business & professional services	Education & health services	Energy	Goods producing	Office using
United States	324.11	0.8%	—	27.2%	2.2%	1.00	2.3%	100%	1.0	10.8%	2.2%	105.2%	109.3%	1.0	1.0	1.0	1.0	1.0
Albuquerque	0.91	0.1%	(0.41)	27.1%	0.6%	0.83	3.7%	92%	0.8	0.9%	2.0%	98.5%	101.5%	1.1	1.0	0.2	0.7	1.0
Atlanta	5.82	1.9%	91.37	27.6%	10.5%	0.97	−3.3%	90%	0.9	8.6%	3.2%	108.5%	114.6%	1.3	0.8	0.6	0.7	1.3
Austin	2.06	3.0%	44.03	31.6%	16.3%	1.03	−7.7%	102%	1.0	6.5%	2.5%	125.9%	133.7%	1.2	0.8	0.5	0.9	1.1
Baltimore	2.81	0.5%	4.53	27.7%	3.8%	1.14	2.8%	106%	1.2	9.7%	1.6%	105.9%	108.2%	1.2	1.2	0.4	0.7	1.1
Birmingham	1.16	0.6%	5.05	26.3%	3.0%	0.85	2.1%	95%	1.0	10.1%	2.4%	100.3%	104.3%	0.9	0.9	0.7	0.9	1.0
Boise	0.69	1.9%	7.96	26.6%	5.9%	0.79	3.7%	85%	0.9	14.9%	2.3%	106.4%	111.5%	1.0	1.0	0.2	1.1	1.0
Boston	4.80	0.7%	15.25	28.4%	2.9%	1.43	3.3%	123%	1.3	11.1%	2.0%	108.2%	111.7%	1.3	1.3	0.5	0.8	1.3
Buffalo	1.13	−0.2%	(3.53)	26.4%	−4.7%	1.20	2.3%	91%	0.9	5.8%	1.3%	104.7%	106.4%	1.0	1.1	1.0	1.0	0.9
Cape Coral/Fort Myers/Naples	1.10	3.7%	43.19	20.6%	14.7%	0.66	−6.3%	94%	1.2	14.8%	4.3%	108.5%	117.9%	0.9	0.8	0.1	0.9	0.9
Charleston	0.75	1.6%	8.27	29.2%	6.3%	0.80	−0.3%	99%	0.9	9.0%	2.3%	112.5%	116.8%	1.1	0.7	0.4	0.9	1.0
Charlotte	2.47	1.8%	42.72	26.8%	12.0%	0.97	−2.6%	90%	0.9	6.0%	2.5%	110.2%	115.4%	1.2	0.7	0.8	1.0	1.2
Chicago	9.61	0.4%	(12.62)	27.9%	2.4%	1.09	3.3%	99%	1.1	11.9%	1.8%	102.2%	105.5%	1.3	1.0	0.9	0.9	1.2
Cincinnati	2.17	0.6%	4.89	26.5%	1.4%	0.97	3.0%	100%	1.0	10.2%	2.3%	104.5%	108.3%	1.2	0.9	1.0	1.1	1.1
Cleveland	2.06	−0.2%	(5.56)	24.6%	−2.2%	1.04	5.9%	98%	1.0	12.7%	1.9%	100.3%	103.6%	1.0	1.2	1.1	1.1	1.0
Columbia	0.83	1.5%	9.56	29.3%	1.3%	0.87	1.5%	93%	0.9	11.4%	2.5%	105.9%	110.9%	0.9	0.8	1.1	0.9	1.0
Columbus	2.04	1.1%	11.91	28.8%	7.1%	1.03	1.8%	96%	1.0	9.7%	2.5%	110.2%	115.5%	1.2	1.0	0.6	0.8	1.2
Dallas/Fort Worth	7.25	2.1%	60.26	18.9%	10.8%	0.78	−5.8%	97%	0.7	10.2%	2.6%	115.8%	123.4%	1.3	0.8	0.7	0.9	1.4
Deltona/Daytona	0.64	2.5%	18.72	21.8%	6.6%	0.54	−1.8%	88%	0.8	11.6%	3.2%	101.4%	107.9%	0.8	1.3	0.2	0.8	0.8
Denver	2.85	1.6%	26.19	28.3%	10.0%	1.13	−0.1%	97%	1.2	11.5%	2.3%	113.9%	120.0%	1.2	0.8	0.8	0.9	1.2
Des Moines	0.62	0.9%	2.11	27.3%	6.6%	1.21	2.4%	85%	1.0	10.2%	1.9%	110.5%	114.3%	1.0	0.8	0.6	0.8	1.4
Detroit	4.30	0.1%	(5.31)	25.1%	0.1%	0.93	4.1%	98%	1.0	16.3%	2.2%	101.3%	105.1%	1.4	1.0	0.7	1.2	1.2
Fort Lauderdale	1.93	1.7%	28.75	25.8%	9.7%	0.84	−1.3%	100%	1.0	12.4%	3.0%	104.4%	110.0%	1.3	0.8	0.2	0.6	1.3
Greenville	0.89	1.4%	9.86	26.5%	2.1%	0.78	1.5%	89%	0.9	10.7%	2.6%	107.8%	112.7%	1.2	0.8	1.8	1.3	1.1
Hartford	1.22	0.4%	2.50	26.4%	0.0%	1.52	5.2%	107%	1.2	8.5%	1.4%	102.7%	105.0%	1.0	1.1	0.4	1.0	1.2
Honolulu	1.00	0.6%	0.35	29.5%	3.3%	1.04	0.5%	162%	1.1	8.3%	1.7%	104.8%	108.1%	1.0	0.9	0.1	0.6	0.9
Houston	6.75	2.0%	75.87	29.0%	9.0%	1.26	−5.4%	101%	1.2	9.4%	1.7%	117.8%	124.5%	1.1	0.8	3.1	1.4	1.0
Indianapolis	2.01	1.0%	9.46	27.2%	6.2%	1.03	3.0%	89%	1.0	14.4%	1.6%	109.0%	112.8%	1.1	0.9	1.2	1.0	1.1
Inland Empire	4.55	1.2%	19.18	29.3%	1.9%	0.65	0.3%	103%	0.7	5.3%	2.5%	106.5%	111.0%	0.8	1.0	0.7	1.0	0.7
Jacksonville	1.47	1.8%	22.43	27.1%	7.8%	0.84	0.8%	94%	1.0	17.8%	3.5%	104.5%	111.0%	1.1	1.0	0.2	0.7	1.2
Kansas City	2.10	0.6%	3.07	26.5%	5.2%	0.96	1.3%	95%	1.0	10.5%	2.2%	105.7%	109.7%	1.2	0.9	0.6	0.8	1.2
Las Vegas	2.17	2.5%	43.59	28.0%	11.9%	0.83	0.2%	93%	0.9	4.8%	4.0%	102.0%	106.0%	1.0	0.6	0.2	0.6	0.9
Los Angeles	10.26	0.7%	(0.76)	30.2%	4.7%	1.17	1.9%	107%	1.0	12.8%	2.3%	104.6%	108.8%	1.0	1.2	0.6	0.8	1.1
Louisville	1.29	0.7%	5.35	25.9%	4.0%	0.93	3.1%	88%	0.9	8.4%	2.4%	107.9%	112.9%	1.0	0.9	0.7	1.2	1.0
Madison	0.64	0.8%	1.92	30.2%	2.0%	1.22	1.4%	98%	1.1	12.9%	2.1%	109.3%	113.8%	0.9	0.8	1.0	0.9	1.0
Memphis	1.36	0.7%	3.13	27.8%	0.6%	0.89	3.4%	90%	1.0	12.6%	2.9%	100.0%	105.1%	1.1	0.9	0.7	0.8	1.0
Miami	2.73	1.3%	28.68	27.2%	9.4%	0.84	0.5%	111%	0.9	13.3%	3.1%	107.9%	113.9%	1.0	1.0	0.3	0.5	1.1
Milwaukee	1.58	0.3%	(2.03)	26.7%	−0.4%	1.03	4.2%	102%	1.1	10.9%	2.2%	100.7%	105.5%	1.1	1.2	0.8	1.3	1.1

Sources: Moody's Analytics, U.S. Census Bureau, Bureau of Economic Analysis, Bureau of Labor Statistics.

* Metro GMP per capita divided by national GMP per capita.

** Cost of doing business: national average = 100 percent.

*** Market per capita disposable income divided by national per capita disposable income.

**** Location quotient measures employment concentration by market: (metro industry employment as a percentage of metro total)/(national industry employment as a percentage of national total).

Exhibit 3-8 Economy

Market	2016 population Total (millions)	2015–2016 % change	5-year annual net migration (000s)	Millennials (age 16–35) % of total population	5-year growth	2016 GMP per capita ratio*	GMP per capita 5-year projected growth	Cost of doing business**	Per capita disposable income ratio***	5-year disposable income growth	Total employment 2015–2016 %change	2016 as % of previous peak	2018 as % of previous peak	Business & professional services	Education & health services	Energy	Goods producing	Office using
United States	**324.11**	**0.8%**	—	**27.2%**	**2.2%**	**1.00**	**2.3%**	**100%**	**1.0**	**10.8%**	**2.2%**	**105.2%**	**109.3%**	**1.0**	**1.0**	**1.0**	**1.0**	**1.0**
Minneapolis/St. Paul	3.57	1.1%	15.77	27.4%	6.4%	1.14	0.7%	105%	1.1	−0.4%	2.2%	106.9%	111.0%	1.2	1.1	0.7	1.0	1.2
Nashville	1.84	1.4%	17.65	28.4%	7.6%	0.98	−2.2%	94%	1.1	11.2%	3.0%	116.7%	122.3%	1.1	1.0	0.5	1.0	1.1
New Orleans	1.27	0.8%	6.35	27.8%	4.5%	0.99	1.2%	89%	1.0	19.9%	−1.4%	105.3%	105.9%	0.9	1.0	1.9	0.8	0.9
New York–Brooklyn	2.66	0.8%	(6.88)	31.7%	11.2%	0.48	−3.6%	135%	0.9	9.6%	1.9%	126.5%	130.4%	0.6	2.3	0.1	0.6	0.9
New York–other boroughs	7.16	0.4%	(5.36)	27.4%	3.3%	0.29	−2.1%	93%	1.0	2.3%	1.6%	109.3%	112.1%	0.8	1.6	0.5	0.8	0.9
New York–Manhattan	1.65	0.3%	(3.48)	35.5%	10.8%	5.06	−3.4%	160%	2.6	8.9%	1.4%	109.6%	112.1%	1.5	0.8	0.0	0.2	1.8
Northern New Jersey	2.52	0.2%	(4.90)	24.8%	2.0%	1.30	6.9%	106%	1.3	13.2%	1.8%	99.1%	102.2%	1.3	0.9	1.5	0.8	1.3
Oakland/East Bay	2.79	1.2%	17.65	27.4%	9.9%	1.07	1.8%	108%	1.3	10.2%	2.8%	105.5%	110.5%	1.2	1.1	0.7	1.0	1.1
Oklahoma City	1.36	0.9%	5.18	29.3%	2.6%	0.92	4.5%	84%	1.0	11.2%	2.1%	111.5%	115.7%	1.0	0.9	2.1	1.0	0.9
Omaha	0.92	1.0%	2.40	27.8%	3.4%	1.04	3.2%	94%	1.1	6.6%	2.0%	108.0%	112.1%	1.1	1.0	0.6	0.9	1.2
Orange County	3.20	0.9%	8.83	28.2%	5.0%	1.40	0.6%	110%	1.2	9.9%	2.5%	104.2%	108.6%	1.3	0.8	0.6	1.2	1.3
Orlando	2.46	3.0%	66.10	29.0%	13.5%	0.95	−4.3%	107%	0.9	15.2%	4.1%	111.1%	119.6%	1.2	0.8	0.2	0.6	1.2
Palm Beach	1.47	2.6%	41.01	22.8%	10.7%	0.81	−4.0%	97%	1.3	19.3%	3.5%	106.3%	113.1%	1.3	1.0	0.1	0.6	1.3
Philadelphia	6.09	0.3%	1.50	27.1%	0.8%	1.07	4.3%	103%	1.2	13.0%	2.0%	102.2%	105.8%	1.1	1.4	0.9	0.8	1.1
Phoenix	4.71	2.4%	82.53	27.6%	8.3%	0.83	−2.4%	98%	0.9	10.2%	4.2%	103.7%	111.5%	1.2	1.0	0.3	0.9	1.3
Pittsburgh	2.36	0.1%	6.78	24.8%	0.5%	1.08	5.8%	98%	1.1	12.8%	1.8%	105.2%	107.8%	1.1	1.3	1.2	1.0	1.0
Portland, ME	0.53	0.4%	1.50	23.4%	1.2%	0.90	3.4%	108%	1.0	1.1%	2.1%	102.6%	105.8%	0.9	1.3	0.6	0.9	0.9
Portland, OR	2.41	1.3%	20.31	27.4%	10.6%	1.37	12.9%	91%	1.0	17.3%	3.0%	109.2%	115.2%	1.1	0.9	0.4	1.2	1.1
Providence	1.62	0.3%	1.87	26.6%	−0.3%	0.90	3.7%	111%	1.0	2.8%	1.4%	100.6%	102.8%	0.9	1.4	0.7	1.0	0.9
Raleigh/Durham	2.52	1.8%	45.42	27.6%	11.4%	0.97	−2.1%	85%	0.9	4.7%	2.9%	109.9%	116.1%	1.2	1.0	0.9	0.9	1.1
Richmond	1.28	0.9%	6.60	27.6%	3.2%	1.07	1.3%	91%	1.0	10.4%	3.0%	105.3%	110.6%	1.1	1.0	0.7	0.7	1.1
Sacramento	2.30	1.2%	16.72	27.9%	4.7%	0.98	2.7%	112%	1.0	9.8%	2.5%	102.3%	106.8%	1.0	1.0	0.2	0.7	0.9
Salt Lake City	1.18	1.3%	2.47	31.0%	3.3%	1.20	7.0%	87%	0.9	14.0%	2.5%	113.4%	118.1%	1.2	0.7	0.9	1.0	1.3
San Antonio	2.41	1.8%	25.67	29.0%	3.9%	0.83	−5.1%	88%	0.9	5.1%	2.6%	119.1%	125.3%	0.9	1.0	0.5	0.8	1.1
San Diego	3.34	1.1%	12.69	31.0%	5.4%	1.16	1.5%	123%	1.1	11.3%	2.5%	107.9%	112.5%	1.2	0.9	0.5	0.9	1.1
San Francisco	1.65	1.0%	8.37	29.7%	16.5%	1.97	−3.3%	121%	1.9	21.8%	1.9%	119.5%	124.3%	1.8	0.8	0.6	0.5	1.7
San Jose	1.99	1.0%	5.43	27.9%	12.1%	1.65	−1.8%	129%	1.6	17.5%	3.3%	119.3%	124.5%	1.5	1.0	0.2	1.4	1.5
Seattle	2.92	1.3%	20.61	28.8%	13.5%	1.57	1.1%	103%	1.4	13.2%	2.6%	111.8%	116.8%	1.1	0.8	0.2	1.2	1.2
Spokane	0.70	1.1%	5.59	26.7%	2.5%	0.86	2.0%	85%	0.9	12.5%	2.2%	105.2%	109.3%	0.8	1.2	0.6	0.9	0.8
St. Louis	2.82	0.2%	0.08	26.3%	1.0%	0.94	3.5%	93%	1.0	12.8%	2.2%	100.7%	104.4%	1.1	1.1	0.9	0.9	1.1
Tacoma	0.85	1.3%	5.61	28.7%	6.9%	0.77	2.3%	90%	1.0	14.1%	2.2%	107.5%	111.6%	0.6	1.2	0.6	0.9	0.7
Tampa Bay/St. Petersburg	3.01	1.7%	53.28	24.5%	7.7%	0.84	−0.7%	101%	0.9	16.8%	3.4%	104.3%	110.2%	1.2	1.0	0.3	0.7	1.3
Tucson	1.04	1.6%	13.09	27.5%	−1.7%	0.74	1.4%	96%	0.8	9.4%	3.4%	99.2%	106.0%	1.0	1.1	0.5	0.8	0.9
Virginia Beach/Norfolk	1.74	0.7%	3.14	30.7%	0.5%	0.99	2.5%	92%	1.0	9.5%	2.3%	100.5%	104.4%	1.0	0.9	0.2	0.9	0.9
Washington, DC–District	0.68	1.2%	2.89	38.2%	15.0%	2.69	−3.7%	120%	1.6	15.1%	1.4%	112.0%	114.8%	1.5	1.1	0.0	0.2	2.5
Washington, DC–MD suburbs	2.31	1.0%	9.59	27.3%	8.1%	0.96	−2.1%	99%	1.2	9.4%	1.1%	102.2%	104.2%	1.3	0.9	0.3	0.7	1.4
Washington, DC–Northern VA	2.96	1.2%	8.84	28.0%	10.7%	1.01	−2.7%	112%	1.3	10.4%	2.1%	108.4%	113.2%	2.0	0.7	0.2	0.5	1.9
Westchester, NY/Fairfield, CT	1.93	0.3%	(1.27)	24.5%	1.0%	1.11	0.0%	125%	1.7	12.9%	1.5%	101.9%	104.3%	1.1	1.2	0.4	0.7	1.2

Exhibit 3-9 Housing

Market	Households		Median home prices				2016 single-family home year-to-year change					Multifamily metrics		
	2016 total (000s)	3-year projected growth	2016 price	2015–2016 % change	2016 as % of peak	Affordability index*	Permits	Starts	Completions	Sales	Walk Score	Rent/cost of ownership**	Rent as % of household income	Space under construction as % of inventory
United States	**123,852**	**4.8%**	**$231,644**	**4.0%**	**104.4%**	**157.48**	**38.2%**	**38.5%**	**24.5%**	**13.8%**	**51**	**0.8**	**31.4%**	**1.4%**
Albuquerque	358	1.8%	$190,834	3.1%	103.8%	166.63	−4.4%	−7.8%	−3.0%	13.5%	40	0.8	26.8%	0.6%
Atlanta	2,139	8.2%	$175,742	2.8%	102.7%	207.88	8.1%	8.9%	8.7%	10.3%	46	0.9	23.2%	2.1%
Austin	780	9.2%	$261,292	1.0%	150.6%	154.42	1.7%	1.7%	−1.8%	13.9%	35	0.7	26.4%	3.2%
Baltimore	1,078	4.1%	$267,943	4.1%	96.0%	168.54	26.5%	26.6%	43.6%	9.4%	66	0.8	26.3%	1.1%
Birmingham	459	4.2%	$180,947	1.4%	109.7%	174.41	−4.8%	−4.5%	−11.7%	8.4%	33	0.7	21.0%	0.5%
Boise	263	7.8%	$197,869	3.4%	97.8%	168.11	32.3%	28.7%	22.4%	17.9%	37	0.7	22.5%	4.8%
Boston	1,860	3.7%	$421,677	3.2%	104.6%	125.18	16.8%	22.3%	34.9%	15.4%	80	0.8	37.6%	1.0%
Buffalo	470	0.7%	$133,313	2.5%	135.5%	275.48	29.0%	36.8%	36.0%	10.3%	65	1.2	26.7%	0.4%
Cape Coral/Fort Myers/Naples	479	15.8%	$337,048	5.5%	80.8%	107.89	33.5%	34.7%	48.8%	15.1%	36	0.6	35.6%	1.3%
Charleston	296	7.3%	$243,238	2.2%	114.7%	149.91	7.1%	8.6%	19.2%	9.5%	34	0.8	30.1%	2.6%
Charlotte	961	8.2%	$207,105	−0.1%	141.4%	166.43	−4.7%	−4.8%	−7.0%	12.7%	24	0.8	26.7%	3.6%
Chicago	3,570	3.0%	$226,848	2.9%	83.3%	175.49	−4.1%	−7.6%	−0.9%	13.0%	75	0.9	29.7%	0.4%
Cincinnati	856	4.1%	$153,344	2.2%	107.5%	235.69	−32.8%	−30.4%	−33.2%	12.8%	50	1.0	24.4%	0.5%
Cleveland	857	1.9%	$128,416	3.2%	96.3%	273.35	41.6%	46.3%	20.2%	11.9%	57	1.1	23.8%	0.2%
Columbia	326	7.0%	$157,232	2.6%	111.8%	214.35	15.4%	16.4%	23.1%	8.4%	35	0.9	25.4%	1.7%
Columbus	808	5.7%	$168,117	1.6%	114.5%	215.38	68.3%	72.9%	24.1%	13.4%	40	0.9	24.2%	1.4%
Dallas/Fort Worth	1,741	8.7%	$220,403	2.5%	138.4%	167.64	1.0%	3.3%	15.6%	14.1%	44	0.9	29.2%	2.7%
Deltona/Daytona	270	11.0%	$160,004	7.3%	77.8%	175.13	93.5%	87.8%	66.0%	13.9%	13	1.0	32.6%	0.5%
Denver	1,147	7.7%	$364,488	4.3%	146.0%	116.64	27.5%	25.7%	23.9%	11.4%	56	0.7	31.5%	2.6%
Des Moines	246	5.7%	$179,098	0.4%	124.0%	222.63	6.8%	6.0%	17.9%	16.3%	42	0.8	21.3%	2.1%
Detroit	1,722	2.8%	$103,931	6.3%	69.3%	348.53	18.8%	23.3%	32.8%	22.7%	52	1.2	18.9%	0.7%
Fort Lauderdale	788	8.2%	$301,874	3.5%	82.3%	108.28	109.3%	108.3%	142.3%	13.8%	54	0.8	42.4%	0.6%
Greenville	361	6.6%	$179,119	2.1%	118.2%	176.54	16.0%	16.8%	20.4%	14.1%	41	0.9	31.7%	2.4%
Hartford	481	2.8%	$247,175	5.2%	96.1%	192.96	33.5%	41.8%	53.7%	13.0%	68	0.8	25.1%	0.4%
Honolulu	330	3.8%	$756,688	1.9%	120.0%	62.66	21.6%	18.3%	18.7%	10.0%	63	0.4	36.1%	0.7%
Houston	2,364	8.5%	$217,964	2.4%	146.2%	161.60	−4.2%	−5.0%	−9.9%	13.2%	44	1.0	30.8%	2.6%
Indianapolis	787	4.4%	$149,715	1.2%	125.8%	231.42	19.6%	28.7%	2.7%	12.3%	29	0.9	23.9%	1.8%
Inland Empire	1,421	7.6%	$303,682	3.3%	75.6%	111.21	54.0%	48.6%	41.6%	12.2%	39	0.7	37.1%	1.0%
Jacksonville	572	8.5%	$202,504	3.3%	105.2%	177.70	28.7%	30.3%	38.4%	13.8%	26	0.7	25.1%	1.3%
Kansas City	836	4.3%	$167,742	1.4%	108.3%	230.24	51.8%	55.8%	17.5%	14.6%	32	0.7	18.2%	1.2%
Las Vegas	809	9.5%	$226,312	4.7%	71.4%	143.06	39.7%	38.3%	22.2%	13.0%	39	0.7	26.2%	1.3%
Los Angeles	3,382	3.7%	$492,913	4.7%	88.5%	71.61	24.3%	21.0%	17.3%	9.7%	50	0.7	54.4%	1.0%
Louisville	526	4.3%	$155,053	2.5%	112.9%	226.95	58.2%	57.4%	44.8%	17.4%	31	0.8	20.8%	0.9%
Madison	272	4.9%	$247,960	2.1%	111.2%	169.59	23.5%	27.5%	29.0%	11.8%	47	0.7	26.8%	1.5%
Memphis	518	4.0%	$150,593	2.8%	105.9%	205.04	30.8%	27.3%	7.0%	8.9%	33	0.8	22.5%	1.1%
Miami	960	6.8%	$291,010	3.5%	77.6%	89.91	63.2%	59.7%	67.7%	13.5%	76	0.9	49.4%	1.6%
Milwaukee	642	3.1%	$219,063	3.0%	99.8%	168.02	43.6%	45.8%	24.9%	11.0%	59	0.7	25.5%	0.3%
Minneapolis/St. Paul	1,422	6.1%	$225,009	1.3%	96.7%	192.06	44.9%	49.2%	45.6%	18.5%	65	0.8	24.3%	1.3%

Sources: U.S. Census Bureau, Moody's Analytics, WalkScore, U.S. Federal Reserve, Reis, CoStar, Bureau of Economic Analysis.
* Affordability is the percentage of the median home price that can be puchased with the median income for the market.
** Market apartment rent divided by median mortgage payment, taxes, insurance, maintenance.

Exhibit 3-9 **Housing**

Market	Households			Median home prices			2016 single-family home year-to-year change					Multifamily metrics		
	2016 total (000s)	3-year projected growth	2016 price	2015–2016 % change	2016 as % of peak	Affordability index*	Permits	Starts	Completions	Sales	Walk Score	Rent/cost of ownership**	Rent as % of household income	Space under construction as % of inventory
United States	**123,852**	**4.8%**	**$231,644**	**4.0%**	**104.4%**	**157.48**	**38.2%**	**38.5%**	**24.5%**	**13.8%**	**51**	**0.8**	**31.4%**	**1.4%**
Nashville	726	6.1%	$200,533	1.9%	114.2%	175.11	7.2%	9.1%	21.4%	10.8%	26	1.0	31.4%	3.0%
New Orleans	495	4.9%	$182,061	2.9%	105.6%	173.77	31.6%	27.7%	−5.9%	10.8%	56	1.0	33.4%	0.4%
New York–Brooklyn	953	4.2%	$453,082	3.5%	103.2%	60.32	21.9%	26.7%	16.4%	12.5%	97	0.8	65.8%	2.1%
New York–other boroughs	2,416	3.3%	$428,327	3.0%	97.4%	89.18	49.3%	53.7%	33.9%	11.2%	83	0.9	51.0%	1.2%
New York–Manhattan	781	2.5%	$1,414,809	3.2%	108.6%	31.28	21.1%	25.9%	16.4%	12.5%	100	0.3	43.0%	1.5%
Northern New Jersey	906	2.6%	$416,623	4.3%	97.0%	125.44	16.5%	22.9%	1.5%	19.1%	78	0.5	26.1%	2.3%
Oakland/East Bay	994	4.3%	$831,416	4.9%	109.9%	64.09	11.3%	11.9%	24.6%	11.6%	69	0.5	45.4%	0.8%
Oklahoma City	530	5.3%	$160,769	1.5%	129.9%	203.43	25.0%	20.0%	−0.5%	12.6%	32	1.0	26.4%	0.9%
Omaha	358	5.2%	$158,541	1.5%	114.8%	230.16	20.9%	25.9%	−2.0%	10.1%	41	1.0	23.7%	1.2%
Orange County	1,057	4.7%	$751,259	3.4%	106.0%	63.42	14.2%	12.4%	35.3%	11.3%	51	0.5	40.8%	1.7%
Orlando	958	13.1%	$202,710	3.5%	75.4%	155.81	39.6%	40.0%	54.2%	15.6%	39	0.8	30.9%	3.1%
Palm Beach	624	11.7%	$314,983	3.1%	82.0%	113.66	69.1%	73.0%	84.4%	14.7%	40	0.8	40.7%	0.7%
Philadelphia	2,322	2.8%	$232,826	3.2%	101.7%	185.76	28.6%	37.2%	27.5%	20.1%	77	0.8	26.9%	1.2%
Phoenix	1,790	10.7%	$226,370	4.2%	84.7%	144.20	27.4%	27.4%	36.4%	10.8%	52	0.7	27.8%	1.8%
Pittsburgh	1,008	0.5%	$148,931	1.9%	129.3%	254.59	96.6%	80.6%	−12.0%	19.6%	60	1.0	25.3%	0.8%
Portland, ME	222	2.9%	$250,545	3.5%	102.7%	150.94	17.5%	23.7%	33.9%	12.9%	63	0.9	36.9%	0.7%
Portland, OR	982	7.0%	$320,580	4.4%	114.5%	125.86	25.8%	24.4%	26.8%	14.6%	57	0.6	28.5%	1.7%
Providence	639	2.0%	$257,146	3.0%	88.2%	147.32	29.3%	35.8%	57.6%	12.8%	76	0.9	35.1%	0.1%
Raleigh/Durham	996	8.7%	$191,884	0.8%	111.9%	192.61	4.0%	3.3%	7.5%	12.8%	29	0.9	27.6%	2.0%
Richmond	502	4.9%	$231,112	2.4%	102.9%	160.58	37.4%	37.0%	35.7%	18.7%	49	0.7	23.4%	1.1%
Sacramento	843	5.4%	$312,593	6.7%	83.6%	125.85	36.7%	36.5%	53.3%	11.1%	33	0.6	28.3%	0.6%
Salt Lake City	395	5.8%	$259,864	3.1%	127.5%	150.12	54.1%	46.2%	32.3%	19.0%	55	0.7	23.8%	3.9%
San Antonio	863	7.7%	$198,246	1.8%	140.3%	162.41	20.9%	21.0%	11.2%	13.5%	34	0.8	25.0%	1.0%
San Diego	1,172	5.1%	$574,481	5.7%	95.7%	72.03	22.5%	26.7%	20.7%	11.2%	49	0.5	41.6%	1.6%
San Francisco	625	3.5%	$1,256,732	4.5%	141.3%	47.94	31.7%	28.3%	32.5%	12.4%	84	0.3	41.0%	1.4%
San Jose	664	4.0%	$1,024,654	5.3%	133.0%	59.42	11.0%	10.5%	9.9%	13.3%	48	0.4	37.8%	2.3%
Seattle	1,175	6.6%	$441,913	4.2%	113.0%	112.73	30.8%	23.7%	4.4%	10.8%	71	0.5	26.3%	2.7%
Spokane	283	5.9%	$198,399	4.2%	102.8%	167.99	1.8%	2.6%	47.2%	10.9%	36	0.7	22.9%	4.2%
St. Louis	1,137	3.0%	$151,300	0.7%	102.7%	247.10	39.0%	48.4%	30.3%	14.2%	60	0.8	19.7%	0.6%
Tacoma	325	6.4%	$248,072	5.1%	96.2%	158.68	30.4%	26.9%	5.9%	9.8%	51	0.9	33.7%	1.0%
Tampa Bay/St. Petersburg	1,272	8.1%	$178,463	5.1%	79.1%	183.31	31.4%	34.5%	50.9%	13.5%	46	0.9	31.0%	1.6%
Tucson	430	8.4%	$196,207	4.9%	80.2%	149.25	28.3%	24.1%	15.4%	9.7%	39	0.7	27.8%	1.0%
Virginia Beach/Norfolk	665	4.6%	$214,806	2.8%	91.7%	165.50	29.6%	29.6%	30.3%	17.6%	38	0.8	26.0%	1.6%
Washington, DC–District	293	4.1%	$377,891	2.0%	101.7%	116.13	5.8%	2.1%	−58.4%	7.9%	74	0.7	33.5%	2.1%
Washington, DC–MD suburbs	841	6.0%	$389,611	1.3%	91.3%	127.95	38.9%	38.9%	54.2%	13.4%	47	0.7	25.5%	0.8%
Washington, DC–Northern VA	1,106	6.3%	$376,357	1.6%	91.1%	139.44	45.3%	48.2%	43.1%	21.3%	56	0.7	25.7%	2.1%
Westchester, NY/Fairfield, CT	697	2.8%	$546,391	4.5%	94.4%	106.20	4.4%	10.1%	100.0%	12.9%	51	0.6	32.6%	0.6%

Exhibit 3-10 West Region: Sector and Local Outlook Scores

Overall rank		Investment prospect scores, by sector						Local outlook score*
		Office	Retail	Industrial	Multifamily	Hotel	Housing	
4	Seattle	3.92	3.80	3.86	3.80	3.61	4.16	4.31
6	Denver	3.62	3.59	3.98	3.75	3.27	4.08	4.23
8	San Francisco	3.71	3.90	3.45	3.86	4.25	4.10	4.31
9	Portland, OR	3.73	3.60	3.74	3.78	3.57	3.45	3.93
10	Los Angeles	3.74	3.82	4.02	3.91	3.74	3.59	3.94
12	San Jose	3.70	3.75	3.63	4.06	3.67	3.78	4.22
14	Orange County	3.62	3.60	3.56	3.93	3.47	3.75	4.02
16	San Diego	3.59	3.61	3.39	3.89	3.53	3.71	3.88
17	Phoenix	3.59	3.50	3.66	3.68	3.02	3.68	3.67
23	Honolulu	2.33	3.69	3.30	3.88	3.30	3.88	3.67
28	Oakland/East Bay	3.26	3.28	3.45	3.50	3.26	3.51	3.92
36	Inland Empire	2.61	3.03	3.94	3.54	2.91	3.64	3.39
42	Salt Lake City	3.17	3.06	3.76	3.10	3.06	3.06	4.21
49	Albuquerque	2.75	3.00	3.25	3.17	3.25	3.33	3.13
54	Boise	2.97	3.18	3.30	3.32	3.05	3.30	3.92
59	Tacoma	3.00	3.58	3.55	3.64	3.04	4.11	4.13
61	Sacramento	3.13	3.27	2.91	3.23	2.91	2.91	3.30
62	Las Vegas	2.66	2.38	3.56	3.38	3.42	3.04	3.60
70	Tucson	2.50	3.50	3.25	3.70	3.00	2.67	3.04
72	Spokane	3.32	3.32	3.32	2.81	2.81	2.81	2.94
33	**West average**	**3.25**	**3.42**	**3.54**	**3.60**	**3.31**	**3.53**	**3.79**

Source: *Emerging Trends in Real Estate 2016* survey.

* Average score of local market participants' opinion on strength of local economy, investor demand, capital availability, development and redevelopment opportunities, public/private investments, and local development community.

City, and Portland. Single-family housing markets expected to outperform the regional average include Seattle, Tacoma, San Francisco, and Denver. Retail markets with the highest outlook scores for 2016 are San Francisco, Los Angeles, Seattle, and San Jose. Survey respondents expect San Francisco, Los Angeles, Seattle, San Jose, and San Diego to be the top hotel markets in the region. Finally, Seattle is projected to be the top West region office market, followed by Los Angeles, Portland, San Francisco, San Jose, Phoenix, and San Diego.

The average local market outlook score for the West region is the highest of all four regions. The markets with the top local outlook scores for 2016 are Seattle, San Francisco, Denver, San Jose, and Salt Lake City.

South Region

The 29 markets that make up the South region have an average rank of 37 in this year's survey. The region is home to Dallas/Fort Worth, the number-one market, and also seven of the top 20 markets.

Survey respondents like the 2016 outlook for housing markets in the South region. The single-family sector has the highest average score of all property types. Markets that are expected to significantly outperform the average include Dallas/Fort Worth,

Exhibit 3-11 **South Region: Sector and Local Outlook Scores**

		Investment prospect scores, by sector						Local outlook score*
Overall rank		Office	Retail	Industrial	Multifamily	Hotel	Housing	
1	Dallas/Fort Worth	3.72	3.82	3.99	3.95	3.72	4.38	4.30
2	Austin	3.85	3.94	3.56	3.91	3.50	4.27	4.28
3	Charlotte	3.73	3.65	3.78	3.68	3.80	4.07	4.12
5	Atlanta	3.84	3.74	3.89	3.67	3.64	3.77	4.02
7	Nashville	3.93	3.65	3.71	3.71	3.45	3.56	4.24
11	Raleigh/Durham	3.62	3.56	3.50	3.58	3.73	3.88	4.17
19	Miami	3.26	3.75	3.56	3.35	3.55	3.33	4.23
20	San Antonio	3.16	3.13	3.37	3.68	3.05	3.83	3.88
24	Washington, DC–District	3.29	3.68	3.28	3.41	3.28	3.47	3.69
25	Charleston	3.25	3.21	3.48	3.35	3.48	3.31	4.18
29	Tampa/St. Petersburg	3.32	3.30	3.44	3.39	3.45	3.46	3.88
30	Houston	2.80	3.56	3.35	3.23	3.28	4.09	3.25
32	Washington, DC–Northern VA	2.96	3.85	3.57	3.65	3.50	3.57	3.43
38	Greenville	3.19	2.89	3.26	3.21	3.23	3.68	4.13
40	Orlando	3.14	3.41	3.34	3.75	3.50	3.31	3.85
41	Fort Lauderdale	3.13	3.36	3.13	3.42	3.36	3.64	4.07
44	Palm Beach	2.82	3.28	3.14	3.55	3.42	3.42	4.09
46	Cape Coral/Fort Myers/Naples	2.94	3.05	2.94	3.70	3.23	3.36	3.50
50	Louisville	2.98	2.98	2.98	3.12	2.55	3.40	3.17
51	Washington, DC–MD suburbs	2.42	3.31	3.36	3.07	3.14	3.36	3.28
52	New Orleans	3.12	3.12	2.83	3.40	2.98	2.98	3.59
53	Jacksonville	2.94	2.90	2.98	3.32	2.93	3.49	3.46
56	Columbia	3.15	3.15	3.15	3.50	3.15	3.15	3.21
60	Oklahoma City	2.76	3.19	3.19	3.40	3.12	2.98	3.59
63	Memphis	2.55	2.98	3.40	2.34	2.55	3.40	3.13
66	Richmond	2.88	2.58	3.25	3.28	3.21	2.88	3.26
67	Birmingham	2.78	2.64	3.32	3.07	2.85	2.95	3.19
69	Virginia Beach/Norfolk	2.29	2.79	2.82	3.07	2.78	2.88	3.28
75	Deltona/Daytona	2.13	2.55	2.98	2.55	2.83	2.55	3.33
37	**South average**	**3.10**	**3.28**	**3.33**	**3.39**	**3.25**	**3.46**	**3.72**

Source: *Emerging Trends in Real Estate 2016* survey.

* Average score of local market participants' opinions on strength of local economy, investor demand, capital availability, development and redevelopment opportunities, public/private investments, and local development community.

Exhibit 3-12 **Local Outlook: South Region**

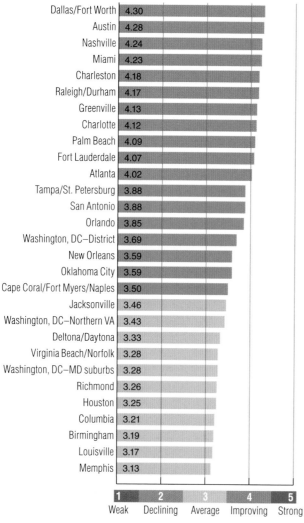

Dallas/Fort Worth	4.30
Austin	4.28
Nashville	4.24
Miami	4.23
Charleston	4.18
Raleigh/Durham	4.17
Greenville	4.13
Charlotte	4.12
Palm Beach	4.09
Fort Lauderdale	4.07
Atlanta	4.02
Tampa/St. Petersburg	3.88
San Antonio	3.88
Orlando	3.85
Washington, DC–District	3.69
New Orleans	3.59
Oklahoma City	3.59
Cape Coral/Fort Myers/Naples	3.50
Jacksonville	3.46
Washington, DC–Northern VA	3.43
Deltona/Daytona	3.33
Virginia Beach/Norfolk	3.28
Washington, DC–MD suburbs	3.28
Richmond	3.26
Houston	3.25
Columbia	3.21
Birmingham	3.19
Louisville	3.17
Memphis	3.13

1 Weak 2 Declining 3 Average 4 Improving 5 Strong

Source: *Emerging Trends in Real Estate 2016* survey.

Note: Average score of local market participants' opinions on strength of local economy, investor demand, capital availability, development and redevelopment opportunities, public/private investments, and local development community.

Austin, Houston, and Charlotte. The multifamily sector is the second-highest-scoring property type in the region. Multifamily markets projected to easily outperform the regional average include Dallas/Fort Worth, Austin, Orlando, Nashville, and Cape Coral/Fort Myers.

After housing, survey respondents like industrial, retail, hotel, and office in the South region. Industrial markets expected to outperform the regional average include the following: Dallas/Fort Worth, Atlanta, Charlotte, and Nashville. Retail markets with the highest outlook score are Austin, northern Virginia, Dallas/Fort Worth, and Nashville. Survey respondents expect Charlotte

Exhibit 3-13 **Local Outlook: Midwest Region**

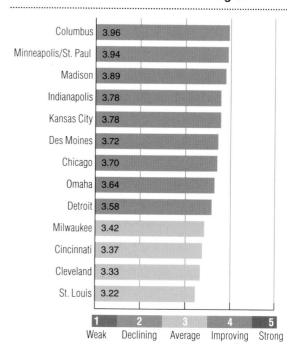

Columbus	3.96
Minneapolis/St. Paul	3.94
Madison	3.89
Indianapolis	3.78
Kansas City	3.78
Des Moines	3.72
Chicago	3.70
Omaha	3.64
Detroit	3.58
Milwaukee	3.42
Cincinnati	3.37
Cleveland	3.33
St. Louis	3.22

1 Weak 2 Declining 3 Average 4 Improving 5 Strong

Source: *Emerging Trends in Real Estate 2016* survey.

Note: Average score of local market participants' opinions on strength of local economy, investor demand, capital availability, development and redevelopment opportunities, public/private investments, and local development community.

to be the top hotel market in the region, followed by Raleigh/Durham, Dallas/Fort Worth, and Atlanta.

The average local market outlook score for the South region is the second highest for all four U.S. regions, trailing only the West region. The markets with the top local outlook scores for 2016 are Dallas/Fort Worth, Austin, Charleston, Nashville, Miami, Raleigh/Durham, and Palm Beach.

Midwest Region

The 13 markets that make up the Midwest region have an average rank of 41 in this year's survey. This ranks the region third out of the four U.S. regions represented. The highest-ranked market in the region is Minneapolis/St. Paul, the only Midwest market represented in this year's top 20.

Survey respondents like the 2016 outlook for industrial markets in the Midwest region. Industrial markets that are expected to significantly outperform the regional average include Detroit, Chicago, and Indianapolis.

After industrial, survey respondents like multifamily, office, retail, single-family housing, and hotel in the Midwest region.

Exhibit 3-14 **Midwest Region: Sector and Local Outlook Scores**

Overall rank		Investment prospect scores, by sector						Local outlook score*
		Office	**Retail**	**Industrial**	**Multifamily**	**Hotel**	**Housing**	
18	Minneapolis/St. Paul	3.47	3.55	3.57	3.76	3.52	3.20	3.94
22	Indianapolis	3.44	3.47	3.68	3.80	3.34	3.20	3.78
26	Chicago	3.58	3.46	3.73	3.77	3.31	3.16	3.70
27	Columbus	3.26	3.02	3.53	3.72	3.41	3.41	3.96
33	Detroit	3.32	3.31	3.73	3.69	3.06	3.12	3.58
34	St. Louis	3.17	3.17	3.67	3.15	2.99	3.56	3.22
39	Kansas City	2.97	3.21	3.53	3.44	2.66	3.23	3.78
45	Cincinnati	3.31	3.07	3.53	3.69	2.91	2.99	3.37
48	Madison	3.21	3.20	3.50	3.34	2.40	2.89	3.89
55	Des Moines	3.08	3.06	3.46	3.50	2.83	2.89	3.72
57	Cleveland	3.47	3.22	3.30	3.70	2.48	2.64	3.33
65	Omaha	2.77	2.88	3.19	3.18	2.53	2.81	3.64
68	Milwaukee	2.98	2.98	3.40	2.83	1.70	2.55	3.42
41	**Midwest average**	**3.23**	**3.20**	**3.52**	**3.51**	**2.86**	**3.05**	**3.64**

Source: *Emerging Trends in Real Estate 2016* survey.

* Average score of local market participants' opinion on strength of local economy, investor demand, capital availability, development and redevelopment opportunities, public/private investments, and local development community.

Multifamily markets expected to outperform the regional average include the following: Indianapolis, Chicago, Minneapolis/St. Paul, Columbus, Cleveland, and Cincinnati. Office markets expected to outperform the regional average include Chicago, Minneapolis/St. Paul, Cleveland, and Indianapolis. Retail markets with the highest outlook scores are Minneapolis/St. Paul, Indianapolis, and Chicago. Survey respondents expect St. Louis, Columbus, and Kansas City to be the top housing markets in the Midwest region. Finally, Minneapolis/St. Paul is projected to be the top Midwest region office market, followed by Columbus and Kansas City.

The average local market outlook score for the Midwest region is the third highest out of the four U.S. regions. The markets with the top local outlook scores for 2016 are Columbus, Minneapolis/St. Paul, Madison, Indianapolis, and Kansas City.

Northeast Region

The 13 markets that make up the Northeast region have an average rank of 45 in this year's survey. This ranks the region number four out of the four U.S. regions represented. Coming in at number 13, the highest-ranked market in the region is Boston.

The Massachusetts state capital is joined by Manhattan as the only two Northeast region markets in this year's top 20.

Survey respondents like the 2016 outlook for retail markets in the Northeast region. Retail markets that are expected to significantly outperform the regional average include Manhattan, northern New Jersey, Brooklyn, Pittsburgh, and New York City's other boroughs.

After retail, survey respondents like multifamily, industrial, single-family housing, hotel, and office in the Northeast region. Multifamily markets expected to outperform the regional average include northern New Jersey, Manhattan, Boston, and Brooklyn. Industrial markets expected to outperform the regional average include northern New Jersey, Baltimore, Boston, Manhattan, and Pittsburgh. Housing markets with the highest outlook scores are Boston, Philadelphia, and Pittsburgh. Survey respondents expect Boston; Portland, Maine; Baltimore; and Pittsburgh to be the top hotel markets in the Northeast region. Finally, Boston is projected to be the top Northeast region office market, followed by Manhattan, Brooklyn, and Pittsburgh.

Exhibit 3-15 Local Outlook: Northeast Region

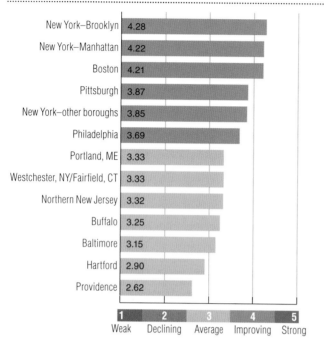

New York–Brooklyn	4.28
New York–Manhattan	4.22
Boston	4.21
Pittsburgh	3.87
New York–other boroughs	3.85
Philadelphia	3.69
Portland, ME	3.33
Westchester, NY/Fairfield, CT	3.33
Northern New Jersey	3.32
Buffalo	3.25
Baltimore	3.15
Hartford	2.90
Providence	2.62

1	2	3	4	5
Weak	Declining	Average	Improving	Strong

Source: *Emerging Trends in Real Estate 2016* survey.

Note: Average score of local market participants' opinions on strength of local economy, investor demand, capital availability, development and redevelopment opportunities, public/private investments, and local development community.

Exhibit 3-16 Northeast Region: Sector and Local Outlook Scores

Overall rank		Investment prospect scores, by sector						Local outlook score*
		Office	Retail	Industrial	Multifamily	Hotel	Housing	
13	Boston	3.82	3.61	3.50	3.70	3.54	3.52	4.21
15	New York–Manhattan	3.64	3.90	3.34	3.81	3.23	3.33	4.22
21	New York–Brooklyn	3.55	3.60	3.36	3.65	3.28	3.25	4.28
31	Philadelphia	3.08	3.45	3.38	3.50	2.87	3.42	3.69
35	Baltimore	2.79	3.47	3.56	3.50	3.39	3.22	3.15
37	Northern New Jersey	2.60	3.70	3.92	3.86	2.99	3.11	3.32
43	Pittsburgh	3.20	3.60	3.30	3.26	3.35	3.30	3.87
47	New York–other boroughs	2.85	3.60	2.95	3.54	2.78	3.09	3.85
58	Westchester, NY/Fairfield, CT	2.76	3.48	2.99	3.31	3.22	3.22	3.33
64	Hartford	2.71	2.83	3.00	3.50	2.80	3.00	2.90
71	Providence	2.69	2.92	3.02	3.05	2.37	2.62	2.62
73	Portland, ME	2.55	3.40	1.70	2.98	3.40	2.55	3.33
74	Buffalo	2.40	2.84	2.59	2.13	2.13	2.54	3.25
45	**Northeast average**	**2.97**	**3.41**	**3.12**	**3.37**	**3.03**	**3.09**	**3.54**

Source: *Emerging Trends in Real Estate 2016* survey.

* Average score of local market participants' opinion on strength of local economy, investor demand, capital availability, development and redevelopment opportunities, public/private investments, and local development community.

Exhibit 3-17 **Local Market Perspective: Development/ Redevelopment Opportunities**

Weak	Declining	Average	Improving	Strong

Portland, ME	4.50	Chicago	3.70
New Orleans	4.50	Phoenix	3.69
Boise	4.50	New York–other boroughs	3.68
Salt Lake City	4.33	Cape Coral/Fort Myers/Naples	3.67
Columbus	4.25	Spokane	3.67
San Antonio	4.24	Cincinnati	3.67
Greenville	4.22	St. Louis	3.65
Raleigh/Durham	4.16	Boston	3.63
New York–Brooklyn	4.16	Jacksonville	3.63
Nashville	4.14	San Diego	3.62
Austin	4.12	Las Vegas	3.60
Denver	4.02	San Francisco	3.60
Dallas/Fort Worth	4.02	Honolulu	3.57
Fort Lauderdale	4.00	Indianapolis	3.56
Louisville	4.00	Philadelphia	3.55
Detroit	4.00	Cleveland	3.50
Madison	4.00	Inland Empire	3.46
Milwaukee	4.00	Washington, DC–District	3.43
Minneapolis/St. Paul	4.00	Deltona/Daytona	3.33
Atlanta	3.98	Tacoma	3.33
Palm Beach	3.92	Providence	3.20
Portland, OR	3.92	Birmingham	3.20
Miami	3.91	Albuquerque	3.17
Tampa/St. Petersburg	3.91	Sacramento	3.17
Des Moines	3.90	Richmond	3.13
Pittsburgh	3.89	Baltimore	3.12
Omaha	3.83	Washington, DC–MD suburbs	3.12
Seattle	3.81	Washington, DC–Northern VA	3.06
Oklahoma City	3.80	Buffalo	3.00
Orlando	3.80	Houston	3.00
Charlotte	3.79	Virginia Beach/Norfolk	3.00
Orange County	3.76	Tucson	3.00
San Jose	3.76	Northern New Jersey	2.88
Charleston	3.75	Westchester, NY/Fairfield, CT	2.86
Oakland/East Bay	3.75	Memphis	2.86
New York–Manhattan	3.75	Hartford	2.75
Los Angeles	3.72	Columbia	2.75
Kansas City	3.70		

Source: *Emerging Trends in Real Estate 2016* survey.

Property Type Outlook

"Optimistic on fundamentals, but prices are testing the resistance level."

Louis Sullivan, the first modern architect, famously wrote that "form follows function." Change over time has altered the mix of functions in all sectors of the U.S. economy. Economic value flows down to the land in ways that are not always immediately obvious. During the first century of our national history, for instance, the United States was predominantly agricultural, with the industrial revolution taking hold principally in a few states along the Atlantic Seaboard. How swiftly and decisively we have changed from being a nation of farmers, to a manufacturing colossus, to an economy of knowledge workers, as Peter Drucker described us.

But, with all that change, the output of agricultural land has exponentially increased. The volume of land in agricultural use remains greater than 900 million acres (1.4 million square miles), or 37 percent of the total land area of the United States. Total output of crops and livestock exceeds $280 billion annually, allowing us to run a trade surplus in farm goods of $28.6 billion in the 12 months ending June 2015. One consequence has been that the value of U.S. farmland has more than tripled (in real dollar terms) since 1970. Economic productivity is the ultimate support for real estate values.

Real estate should not fear technologies. While there are bound to be winners and losers, technology's most significant contribution is to ensure that competition in the world of real estate assets is not necessarily a zero-sum game. Economically valuable technologies increase the size of the pie by expanding output: that is the "function" side of things.

As far as "form" goes, the amazing thing is how adaptable real estate actually turns out to be. We are by now quite familiar with adaptive use in the form of lofts to housing, or offices to hotels. No doubt there will be new shifts in highest and best use as

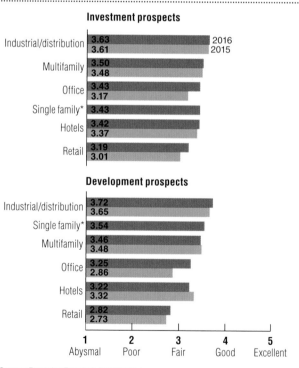

Exhibit 4-1 Prospects for Major Commercial Property Types, 2016 versus 2015

Source: *Emerging Trends in Real Estate* surveys.
* First year in survey.
Note: Based on U.S. respondents only.

existing properties adapt their physical design to new functional needs. The opportunistic move will often be to alter form to accommodate improved functioning. The very gist of positive feasibility is an acknowledgment that the new form and function exceed the value of a previous use.

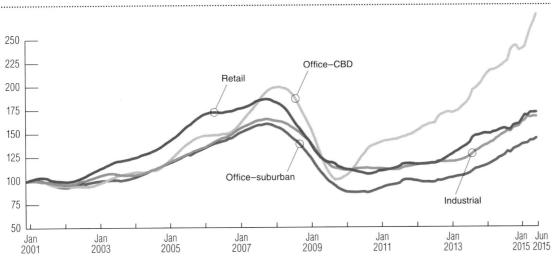

Exhibit 4-2 **Moody's/RCA Commercial Property Price Index, by Sector**

Sources: Moody's and Real Capital Analytics.

Note: Updated August 2015; data through June 2015.

The market reflects this basic economic principle as it allocates capital. Capital allocation, in turn, prices the various economic uses as expressed in the expected return. In many places, trends will still drive activity toward sites where the land has a low basis, and for this reason the interviewees who believe that "the suburbs are not dead" can be vindicated. But for other places, most notably the 24-hour and 18-hour cities, highest and best use is best realized by increased density.

Remarkably, this explains why real estate can at the same time be considered as a fixed asset, but also behave as one of the most dynamic and innovative forms of capital.

Industrial

We are a knowledge-driven society and a knowledge-driven economy whose innovations and growth are based on a Moore's Law technology curve. It is a "creative class" economy where more attention is paid to apps than to appliances, where artificial intelligence is more interesting than hands-on knowledge, where algorithms trump the lessons of praxis.

Yet, over time, the American economy has become more and more an economy that is about "stuff." Look to the truck congestion on our highways and the containers flowing through our ports for tangible evidence. Measure the shift in consumption expenditures from the low 60 percent of gross domestic product (GDP) range that typified the 1960s to today's approximately 70 percent. Look at the annualized growth of retail sales, which has outstripped GDP growth throughout the most recent eco-

nomic recovery. While manufacturing employment has indeed declined, real (inflation-adjusted) output from U.S. industry is now 85 percent greater than in 1987.

Such trends have not been lost on the real estate industry. "Secular trends are goosing demand," in the words of one institutional investment manager.

Enthusiasm for the industrial property type is manifest. A public pension fund manager sees industrials with "a longer runway for appreciation and income growth because of the economic landscape in this country." The senior asset manager for a global fund said, "I'm bullish on industrials." And the chief executive of an investment management firm succinctly put it thusly: "Industrials rule."

The basic motivations are relatively easy to understand: Investors like the value-for-price relationship in a property type where the average cap rate is 6.9 percent. They like the downside protection afforded by the triple-net leases that are typical in this sector. They like the cash-in-hand quality of industrials. National Council of Real Estate Investment Fiduciaries (NCREIF) data show recent capital appreciation at an 8.1 percent annual rate.

The results of the *Emerging Trends* survey not only place industrials at the top of the commercial property sector for investment and development prospects next year in 2016, but also posted the highest score achieved for industrial properties in our surveys as tracked since 2004.

Exhibit 4-3 Prospects for Commercial/Multifamily Subsectors in 2016

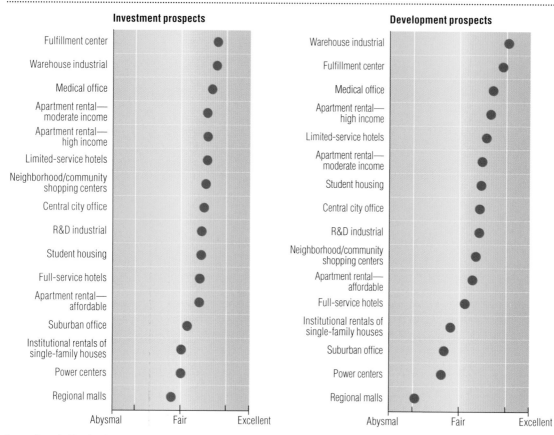

Investment prospects

	Abysmal	Fair	Excellent
Fulfillment center			
Warehouse industrial			
Medical office			
Apartment rental—moderate income			
Apartment rental—high income			
Limited-service hotels			
Neighborhood/community shopping centers			
Central city office			
R&D industrial			
Student housing			
Full-service hotels			
Apartment rental—affordable			
Suburban office			
Institutional rentals of single-family houses			
Power centers			
Regional malls			

Development prospects

	Abysmal	Fair	Excellent
Warehouse industrial			
Fulfillment center			
Medical office			
Apartment rental—high income			
Limited-service hotels			
Apartment rental—moderate income			
Student housing			
Central city office			
R&D industrial			
Neighborhood/community shopping centers			
Apartment rental—affordable			
Full-service hotels			
Institutional rentals of single-family houses			
Suburban office			
Power centers			
Regional malls			

Source: *Emerging Trends in Real Estate 2016* survey.

Note: Based on U.S. respondents only.

Our industry consensus believes that supply/demand fundamentals are sound for the sector. The lead researcher for a large brokerage says, "Actually, we will see a pickup in absorption as some of this industrial space completes, just because people are having trouble finding the product they want. Even with all this new supply coming on the industrial front, we think there is a wave of absorption that comes with it." A major life company asset manager endorses that viewpoint: "We're seeing good, strong demand. There is new construction, but it seems to be being absorbed at the pace that it's being built." A global asset manager agrees, saying, "With the warehouse distribution for [online retailers] combined with the traditional, I think there is going to be a lot of demand."

That demand is itself fairly diverse. Technology, seen as disruptive to real estate by many, has been a positive influence on the industrial real estate sector. The internet has been a major driver as e-commerce has expanded the need for fulfillment centers. Survey respondents were given fulfillment centers as

an industrial segment category for the first time this year, and rated that segment above warehouse/distribution and R&D/flex for investment potential in 2016. A prominent consultant urges a look at "industrial in the new economy." He says, "Warehouse facilities for the new economy are the new retail; they bypass the retail channel and go directly to consumer from warehouse."

Emerging Trends interviewees distinguish between the macro patterns and the on-the-ground differences in facilities' size and local market configurations. "You've seen construction in large space, but we haven't built as much small space [under 200,000 square feet]. There is a real shortage in that area, and that is usually the product that is fairly close in. So as we look to same-day delivery, those smaller warehouses are what you need, close to the urban center." We have heard a lot about the "smile states" (the two coasts linked by the Sun Belt), but there are investors examining opportunities other than ports and bulk distribution. One investment banker observes, "Industrial in the right spot is still a very attractive segment. The corridor from

Exhibit 4-4 Prospects for Niche and Multiuse Property Types in 2016

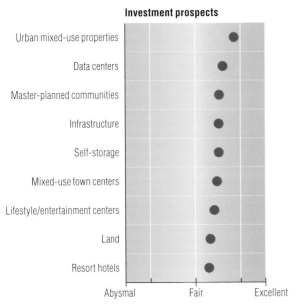

Investment prospects

Urban mixed-use properties	
Data centers	
Master-planned communities	
Infrastructure	
Self-storage	
Mixed-use town centers	
Lifestyle/entertainment centers	
Land	
Resort hotels	

Abysmal · Fair · Excellent

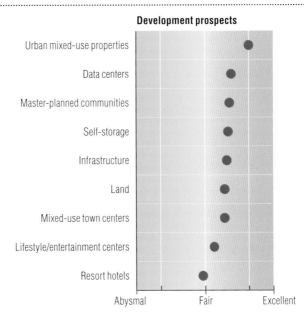

Development prospects

Urban mixed-use properties	
Data centers	
Master-planned communities	
Self-storage	
Infrastructure	
Land	
Mixed-use town centers	
Lifestyle/entertainment centers	
Resort hotels	

Abysmal · Fair · Excellent

Source: *Emerging Trends in Real Estate 2016* survey.

Note: Based on U.S. respondents only.

Exhibit 4-5 U.S. Industrial Property Total Returns

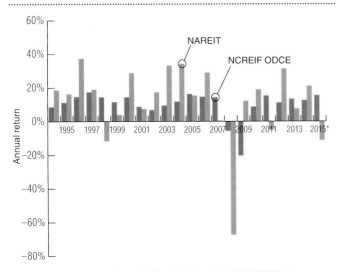

NAREIT

NCREIF ODCE

Sources: NCREIF Fund Index Open-End Diversified Core (ODCE); NAREIT Equity REIT Index.

* Returns as of June 30, 2015.

Milwaukee to the Wisconsin/Illinois border has seen tremendous growth in the industrial area." That perspective is echoed by a private equity executive who favors light industrials in infill locations. First-quarter 2015 data from NCREIF showed the

Exhibit 4-6 Change in Supply and Demand—U.S. Industrial

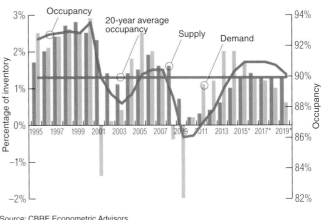

Occupancy

20-year average occupancy

Supply

Demand

Source: CBRE Econometric Advisors.

* Forecast.

Midwest with the highest total returns in industrials among all U.S. regions.

Construction is definitely accelerating in this sector, but it is coming off a lengthy period of virtually no development at all. So attention to high year-over-year change is less meaningful than consideration of the absolute amount of new space being provided in the vast (about 14 billion square feet) national industrial

Exhibit 4-7 Industrial/Distribution Investment Prospect Trends

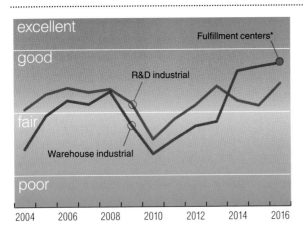

Source: *Emerging Trends in Real Estate* surveys.

* First year in survey.

U.S. warehouse industrial

2016	Prospects	Ranking
Investment prospects	3.78	2
Development prospects	4.04	1

Buy 54.4%	Hold 26.9%	Sell 18.8%

Expected capitalization rate, December 2016	6.1%

U.S. R&D industrial

2016	Prospects	Ranking
Investment prospects	3.45	9
Development prospects	3.42	9

Buy 31.3%	Hold 42.4%	Sell 26.4%

Expected capitalization rate, December 2016	6.7%

U.S. fulfillment centers

2016	Prospects	Ranking
Investment prospects	3.80	1
Development prospects	3.92	2

Buy 44.2%	Hold 40.6%	Sell 15.2%

Expected capitalization rate, December 2016	6.1%

Source: *Emerging Trends in Real Estate 2016* survey.

Note: Based on U.S. respondents only.

property market. Those who are nervous about incipient over-supply seem to focus on the growth rate, absent a longer-term perspective, or are worried by past patterns to continue building

past the cyclical peak in demand. Meanwhile, they observe the prior weighting toward build-to-suit industrial shifting toward the more familiar area of speculative construction.

The multiyear period of supply discipline should not breed complacency, though, especially for industrial assets where the development period is exceptionally short. As one institutional investment manager exclaimed, "Supply constraint? Really?" It is true that the past five years are not likely to be a good guide to the next five, and industrial construction is one area to watch vigilantly.

Two additional considerations should be highlighted: The first is the rotation forward of investor appetite for R&D/flex space, both by owner-users (particularly the big Silicon Valley brand names) and by traditional investors from the institutional and private equity sectors. The second is the targeting of industrial property portfolios as a way to put money to work at scale by sovereign wealth funds, real estate investment trusts (REITs), and pension funds.

In the more globalized, institutionalized real estate environment, size *does* matter, especially in the efficiency of capital deployment. However, we should have already learned that when the big guys concentrate on the biggest assets in the biggest markets, that opens up viable niches elsewhere. Entrepreneurs have often nimbly seized such opportunities, in the computer field, in transportation, and in finance as well. A niche-sensitive investment ecology will shape real estate trends over the foreseeable future.

Apartments

The highly favored multifamily rental sector has enjoyed a long run of success during this decade. Our *Emerging Trends* survey respondents still rate its prospects well, yet the extraordinarily high prices and low cap rates in many locations are giving quite a few of our interviewees pause as they contemplate the future. We may well be seeing the beginning of a shift in investment/development outlook as we go forward in 2016 and later. The executive vice president of a major national developer remarked, "I have never seen the apartment sector so good. That will change. There is too much building in some markets. High rent increases will have to come down." A private equity manager observed, "This is a great market to sell. Investing is more challenging."

Too often, issues in this sector are conflated in an attempt to draw a broadly sketched picture. The urban/suburban choice, for instance, is frequently identified with the rent/buy choice, and that's just not the case. An investment banker told us, "The question is now: do people want to own a house, or do they want to live in the city and rent an apartment? Is property ownership still a main trend?" Many couch the discussion in such a framework. But, for residential investment, a huge range of options means that there are selections for investors and developers in all products. A fine-grained look in this sector is not only essential analytically, but also the key for those who need to pull the trigger on deals.

An analyst with one of the major housing data firms believes that the size of generation Y ("a very interesting cohort") should support expanding housing demand for both rentals and ownership housing. It is not an either/or proposition. "The demographic forces are very positive to support residential construction, support multifamily, while serving a growing need for additional single-family housing stock."

Garden apartments. Institutions have enjoyed a "golden era" in the apartment market. Robust leasing activity has continued in 2015, pushing occupancy and rent growth higher even as multifamily development accelerated swiftly. NCREIF has reported double-digit total returns continuing, with the garden apartment subsector moving ahead of higher-density residential, largely on the strength of superior net operating income (NOI) growth.

According to a midyear 2015 report by Real Capital Analytics, the garden apartment sector is also seeing stronger investment volume growth in the transaction data. While the pressure of institutional investment competition in this recovery has inexorably pushed cap rates lower for mid- and high-rise multifamily assets, garden apartments have maintained average cap rates above 6 percent, compared with mid-/high-rise going-in rates that average 4.9 percent.

Some adopt the Baseball Hall of Famer "Wee" Willy Keeler's advice: "Keep your eye on the ball and hit 'em where they ain't." A West Coast investment manager reported an investment program on Florida's Gulf Coast—still rebounding from the subprime mortgage crisis—where good-quality apartment complexes have been acquired at 7.5 percent cap rates at prices in the $50,000 to $75,000 per unit range. So with many echoing the financier who told us, "Values in New York and San Francisco are just ridiculous," we see a trend in finding multifamily housing opportunities where costs are more manageable, looking more favorably to the garden apartment subsector.

Urban multifamily. For some investors, the best tactical approach means taking profits in a market that will still be strong in 2016, and redeploying the capital into preferred assets. A Wall

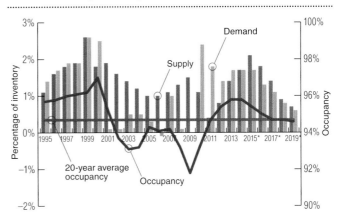

Exhibit 4-8 Change in Supply and Demand— U.S. Multifamily Housing

Source: REIS Inc.

* Forecast.

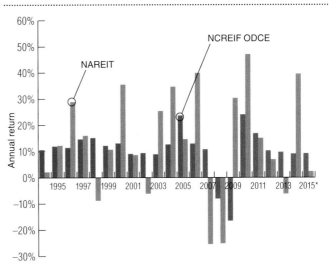

Exhibit 4-9 U.S. Multifamily Property Total Returns

Sources: NCREIF Fund Index Open-End Diversified Core (ODCE); NAREIT Equity REIT Index.

* Returns as of June 30, 2015.

Street fund manager comments, "Our portfolio has very much evolved. We are selling out of the older-style apartments at very high prices and replacing them with newer and much more urban properties in the seven or eight target markets where we can create scale." A public pension fund investor calls luxury apartments in urban infill areas the "best bet" for 2016: "We love the big three [Manhattan, San Francisco, Los Angeles] and we also like the multifamily markets in Seattle, Dallas, and Atlanta."

Exhibit 4-10 Apartment Investment Prospect Trends

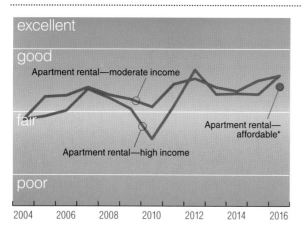

Source: *Emerging Trends in Real Estate* surveys.

* First year in survey.

U.S. high-income apartments

2016	Prospects	Ranking
Investment prospects	3.58	4 (tie)
Development prospects	3.66	4

Buy	Hold		Sell
21.0%	25.7%		53.4%

Expected capitalization rate, December 2016	4.9%

U.S. moderate-income apartments

2016	Prospects	Ranking
Investment prospects	3.58	4 (tie)
Development prospects	3.48	6

Buy	Hold	Sell
38.8%	37.4%	23.8%

Expected capitalization rate, December 2016	5.6%

U.S. affordable apartments

2016	Prospects	Ranking
Investment prospects	3.40	12
Development prospects	3.28	11

Buy	Hold	Sell
32.9%	45.2%	21.9%

Expected capitalization rate, December 2016	6.1%

Source: *Emerging Trends in Real Estate 2016* survey.

Note: Based on U.S. respondents only.

Others, such as the president of a Southeast brokerage, also encourage a close look at what is going on in the regional markets with which he is familiar. "Downtown housing has more of a boutique feel than in New York. Millennials here can rent

affordably at incomes of $125,000." This interviewee went on to mention that this group's downtown experience has led to interest in close-in for-sale housing as a next step. And as for the proposition that educational choices will drive millennials to traditional suburbs eventually, he notes that charter schools and homeschooling have expanded educational choice: neither needs the traditional suburb to be successful.

While many other interviewees still view schools as the stumbling block to city living (as one institutional investor argued, "Unless you can fix the school system in urban areas, as much as millennials say they'll never go to the suburbs, when they have children they probably will"), others concur with the position stated in the previous paragraphs ("I definitely don't think you'll find [gen Y] moving for a school district; they might find a magnet school," as a seasoned appraiser-consultant said in her interview).

Infill and mixed-use development. With the evolution of 18-hour cities, more places around the country are benefiting from additional diversity and complexity in their populations and economic bases. A Tennessee developer lauds the planning trend to rethink "separation of uses" zoning. He believes that "it is smart to seek an environment where something is going on every night." Mixed-use development in such a context reinforces value across the varied uses. An executive with a retail REIT concurs, "Infill and MXD [mixed-use development] are megatrends, and horizontal MXD is easier than vertical. It is more efficient, too, since you have greater cross-use of the parking requirement over the course of the day."

A New York–based firm that intermediates cross-border investment has been doing ground-up apartment development in spots like Altamont Springs outside Orlando; Revere, Massachusetts, near Boston; and the Clayton suburb near St. Louis. "We see these as infill locations, too, not sprawl at the perimeter—and our projects have been exceeding pro-forma projections."

Residual impact of the bubble years. Quite a hangover remains from the U.S. housing market collapse, epitomized by the subprime mortgage–induced bubble a decade ago. More than 7.4 million homeowners are still seriously underwater as of mid-2015, with the market value of the homes 25 percent or more lower than the outstanding mortgage balance, according to Realty Trac. Based on such data, a Wall Street finance specialist sees a slow recovery in the suburban housing markets and a disincentive for homebuying for now.

Such conditions surely influence the buy/rent decision. Many have spoken of the trauma felt by millennials who saw their families' net worth evaporate in the housing debacle. Those scars, they feel, will be very slow to heal. Moreover, the tenuous situation they experience in terms of job security gives them pause when contemplating a long-term mortgage commitment. "Jobs are not 'sticky' anymore," declares an executive with a global investment and asset manager, "and this impacts on the home purchase and mortgage decision."

With such factors in mind, many long-term investors align with an institutional investor who concludes for the years ahead, "We are still bullish on the apartment sector, although there are certainly markets with emerging supply issues. Overall, we think that the **demographic tailwind for rental apartments and continued urbanization is a longer-term trend that will make multifamily a good sector for a long time."**

Design, price, and user preferences. A Chicago-based developer described the difference between product for millennials and baby boomers this way: "The gen Y product is a 700-square-foot apartment at $2,000 per month, but empty nesters need 1,500 square feet." This is another instance where granular market analysis is absolutely required.

Lest we think this is simply the case in the largest U.S. cities, listen to a Nashville housing investor/developer: "My key demographic is women in their 60s, whose social life centers on their jobs and their church affiliations. They need a low-maintenance home with enough size and community amenity to be happy at this stage in life. The micro unit is not the answer for this group." And a West Coast investor wonders about the durability of the market for such a product: "When people are successful, they don't want to be crammed into micro units."

So even as we see a push in demand coming from new household formation, as jobs become more plentiful and release "boomerang" kids into the housing market, there will be a need for a range of development—not just luxury. A challenge for the industry is making the economics of affordable housing work. As one investment manager noted, both ends of the income inequality spectrum need to be satisfied: "We need to ask where workers will be living."

One consultant from the Carolinas maintains, "We are going to have to deal with affordable housing in a more holistic way." A private developer in Florida defines the issue even more sharply: **"Affordable housing is much more than simply a real estate issue. It is a significant cultural issue. Products will be delivered that will accommodate millennials, small/ young families, workforce housing—and how that housing changes . . . in size of home, style of home, where they are located, and how they're constructed."**

That challenge will not be going away in 2016, 2017, or 2018. It is safe to label it an "emerging trend."

Office

Mind the gap! That's the gap between CBD and suburban offices, the top and bottom lines respectively in Moody's/RCA Commercial Property Price Index in exhibit 4-2. One property type diverging on two separate tracks—and the gap has been widening.

The breadth of the U.S. office market is one of its greatest strengths. Having options provides value. Secondary office markets are experiencing higher levels of investment for just this reason, somewhat greater volatility priced by higher yields, and the ability to accommodate fast-growing companies with a volume of new construction at costs much lower than that available in the primary downtowns. Interviewees spoke of "pocket markets," conversions and redevelopments, and opportunities to reposition struggling suburban office parks with vast parking into more effective mixed use.

Where? Quite a few interviewees find themselves overweighted in office at this stage of the cycle. Almost universally, that concentration of investment has been in the downtowns of the largest cities. Research has validated the claims that 24-hour cities would provide superior returns over time. New studies of "vibrancy" have extended the connection between live/work/play locations and commercial real estate performance into the category of 18-hour cities introduced in *Emerging Trends 2015*.

Institutional investors with a long-range perspective have been looking past the high prices for core office assets in gateway markets, doubling down on offices in Boston, Chicago, D.C., New York, Los Angeles, and San Francisco. Even at higher prices, CBD has topped suburban office in total returns over the one-, three-, five-, ten-, and 20-year time horizons in the NCREIF Property Index. No wonder that one interviewee specializing in office investment sales said, **"Tenants want to be in urban locations, so investors want to be there, too.** There is a good degree of due diligence being done on deals, so we are not getting out over our skis."

It is not just the insurance companies and pension funds, though. A variety of buyer types is represented in the current wave of downtown office acquisitions. A private owner/investor told us, "Sell noncore assets; invest in quality office." One inter-

Exhibit 4-11 U.S. Office Property Total Returns

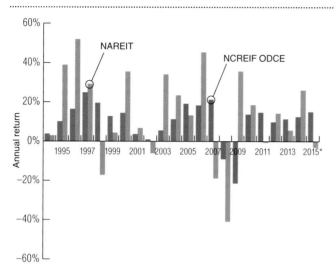

Sources: NCREIF Fund Index Open-End Diversified Core (ODCE); NAREIT Equity REIT Index.
* Returns as of June 30, 2015.

Exhibit 4-12 Change in Supply and Demand—U.S. Office

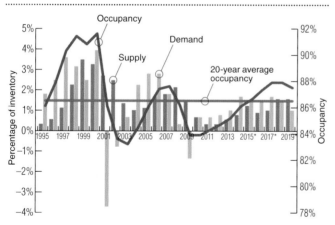

Source: CBRE Econometric Advisors.
* Forecast.

viewee cited the move of a forest products firm from its longtime suburban campus to Seattle's gritty Pioneer Square, remarking, "Companies are all competing for talent. How are you going to attract the talent right out of college? The CBD is benefiting from the trend of companies moving from the suburbs into the center city." Such a reversal of the corporate migration patterns that dominated relocation decades ago, patterns that made suburbanization more than just a residential phenomenon, suggests that the back-to-the-city movement may be with us for a while yet.

Exhibit 4-13 Office Investment Prospect Trends

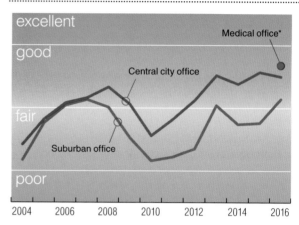

Source: *Emerging Trends in Real Estate* surveys.
* First year in survey.

U.S. central city office

2016	Prospects	Ranking
Investment prospects	3.50	8
Development prospects	3.43	8

Buy 32.7%	Hold 34.6%	Sell 32.7%

Expected capitalization rate, December 2016   5.6%

U.S. suburban office

2016	Prospects	Ranking
Investment prospects	3.14	13
Development prospects	2.67	14

Buy 24.4%	Hold 39.7%	Sell 35.9%

Expected capitalization rate, December 2016   6.9%

Medical office

2016	Prospects	Ranking
Investment prospects	3.68	3
Development prospects	3.71	3

Buy 40.4%	Hold 37.3%	Sell 22.3%

Expected capitalization rate, December 2016   6.4%

Source: *Emerging Trends in Real Estate 2016* survey.
Note: Based on U.S. respondents only.

Of course, here again it is prudent to warn against overgeneralization. More than a few interviewees caution that the suburbs are not dead, and economic equilibrium should mean that the gap in rents and prices between the gateway market downtowns and their nearby suburbs cannot expand indefinitely. At some point, a price advantage stimulates demand.

That countertrend is already quietly underway. First-half 2015 transaction data put suburban office sales volume at $39.8 billion, versus $31.6 billion for CBD office. Both in southern California and the Bay Area, suburban office sales were in the billions, led by Silicon Valley. Similarly, Seattle's suburbs saw $1.8 billion in investment. This is not just a West Coast story. Boston, New Jersey, and the northern Virginia suburbs of Washington, D.C., also broke the billion-dollar barrier. And so did Sun Belt suburbs around Atlanta, Dallas, Denver, and Phoenix.

Costs count. An interviewee whose firm is closely associated with high-rise urban office properties wondered, **"At what point does the cost of living in some cities—driven by housing expense—cut off the flow of young employees? I need to think about places with a more manageable cost of living, secondary markets—Pittsburgh, Minneapolis, Austin.** You give up the excitement of Manhattan or San Francisco, but something's gotta give." It is always healthy when a thoughtful sense of limits enters the discussion of market trends.

Drawing a bright line between all downtowns and all suburbs probably does not make sense. A value-add investor describes his firm's approach this way: "We are conservative in core markets and looking for opportunities in second-ring urban neighborhoods. We are focused on urbanizing suburbs." That means places with a historic retail core on Main Street, with mixed-use potential, but without the high density of the true urban experience. Other interviewees were enticed by "close-in suburbs," with great attention to submarket distinctions, while dismissing the plain-vanilla suburban business park: "They have nothing. There is no reason for people to be there," in the words of a major private equity executive. A specialist in the commercial real estate debt markets says, in contrast, "Suburban office needs to be near transit or walkable to be viable."

How? Costs are very much part of the densification discussion, and space compression is still trending in the minds of many. But here, too, we find some sense of limits, and greater nuance in the thinking of building owners and managers as the actual operation of redesigned space is fleshed out by experience.

"The buildout is actually more expensive if you do it right," said one senior officer about an installation that combined open-space planning with other functional elements. "Somebody who needs private time for calls, for writing, needs a place to go. You end up with a lot of glass and a lot of light. You have open

space, drop-in space, meeting space, some offices. If you do it right, it increases productivity. If you do it cheaply, you run into problems."

A Texas developer sketched out an office property he had repositioned as "millennium space, people stacked in 50 square feet each. But then you go back and look at the common space and see it is not so much a difference in the quantity of space as in the uses of that space. There was a Zen room, space to go mellow out. I imagine after sitting next to someone five feet away you might need a space like that, what I would call common nonfunctioning space."

Productivity and employee experience are both design values in the densification discussion. The concept is not space reduction for its own sake, in most cases. It is about collaboration and interaction. "It's about attracting the talent," said the manager of a Seattle firm. "Companies want to induce interactions and, lo and behold, people are happier. Attract and retain talent." That's good business. Form follows function.

Another seasoned building owner thinks it comes back to the venerable economic concept of agglomeration, and considers the technological revolution an ally to real estate investors. "Technology has been very good for office—net, net, net. Access to high-speed connections caused people to cluster where those connections exist. More and more of the world is on a screen, but **you only really make money on information that is *not* out in the market. That's why people in Silicon Valley want to have lunch in little pubs. Tech has made person-to-person interaction—privately—way more valuable."**

Why? How does this translate into a bottom line? Employers talk about building a culture of collaboration, liberating the workday from the 9-to-5 limits and keeping workers in the workplace longer (as well as closer). Again, the issue is productivity: Does being in the office for 12 hours translate into 12 hours of work, or just eight hours of output? There has recently been pushback. One interviewee maintains, "At some point, the novelty will wear off." An institutional investor believes, "We are going to see the pendulum swing back a little on this dense open-office configuration. I'm hearing more and more evidence that some of the new dense-space configurations are simply less productive than those that do have more privacy."

Like every emergent trend, densification will either prove its worth over time, or it won't. Most probably, the very large office market provides plenty of options along the space/design spectrum, and individual firms will demand varying designs for their spaces. One interviewee, an investment banker, observed that it was the technology, advertising, media, and information (TAMI) firms that were driving office demand, not the finance, insurance, and real estate (FIRE) companies that were once the mainstays. Does that mean buildings without large floor plates? Look no further than the new World Trade Center complex in Manhattan, built with the kind of floor plates that could have facilitated trading operations. Those buildings are now the center of the lower Manhattan TAMI beehive.

There is a lot of room for change. Some see steady growth ahead in the medical office field, recognizing that we are just at the beginning of the aging of the baby boomers. Both private equity firms and more institutional players are seeing the need for more suburban medical office development and even large-scale medical campuses as the health care industry consolidates. The provision of insurance to millions of additional Americans under the Affordable Care Act actually appears to be accelerating health care consolidation, for reasons of economies of scale, while simultaneously creating small-space demand for medical offices specializing in urgent care. Such trends create options for real estate development and investment, for those nimble enough to take advantage. There are gaps to be found—not only in pricing, but also in the matching of supply to demand.

Hotels

A rising U.S. dollar is making international travel to the United States more costly for tourists and business visitors. Airbnb is seen as diverting demand from full-service hotels. The recent surge in development in the hospitality industry is challenging the hotel sector to keep occupancy and revenue per available room (RevPAR) numbers robust, though RevPAR is up again in mid-2015 as it has been each year since 2010.

Emerging Trends survey respondents seem to expect 2016 to be an inflection point for the hotel sector, especially for full-service facilities. Let's be clear that the overall development/investment outlook for both of those segments is up from the survey scores a year ago. That's good. But the percentage of respondents favoring a "sell" posture has risen since our last survey for limited-service hotels, and for full-service hotels there is a higher proportion of "sell" recommendations (30.7 percent) than "buy" (24.8 percent).

According to Real Capital Analytics, capital flows into hotels have remained high during the first half of 2015, at $26.9 billion, 70 percent of which was directed to full-service facilities. These larger and more prestigious assets were favored by offshore investors and by the publicly owned operating companies.

Exhibit 4-14 **Change in Supply and Demand—U.S. Hotel/Lodging**

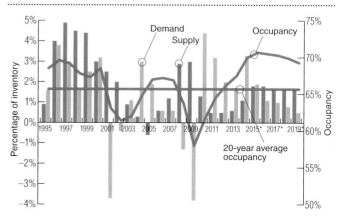

Source: CoStar Portfolio Strategy.
* Forecast.

Exhibit 4-15 **U.S. Hotel/Lodging Property Total Returns**

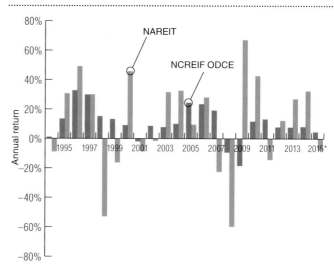

Sources: NCREIF Fund Index Open-End Diversified Core (ODCE); NAREIT Equity REIT Index.
* Returns as of June 30, 2015.

Private equity funds and the REITs, meanwhile, were buyers of limited-service portfolios, to a greater degree.

Hotels have always been understood as more of an operating business than most other forms of real estate. Volatility is always the norm because the "lease term" is by-the-night, with fluctuations in both room rate and occupancy occurring on a daily basis. That can be good when the markets are tight, as they have been. But it is a risk when an increase in supply, which

Exhibit 4-16 Hotel Investment Prospect Trends

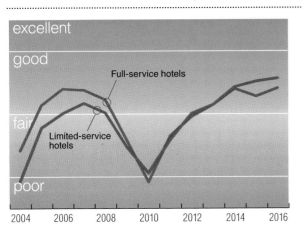

Source: *Emerging Trends in Real Estate* surveys.

U.S. limited-service hotels

2016	Prospects	Ranking
Investment prospects	3.57	6
Development prospects	3.57	5

Buy 31.4%	Hold 40.2%	Sell 28.4%

Expected capitalization rate, December 2016	7.4%

U.S. full-service hotels

2016	Prospects	Ranking
Investment prospects	3.41	11
Development prospects	3.12	12

Buy 24.8%	Hold 44.6%	Sell 30.7%

Expected capitalization rate, December 2016	7.0%

Source: *Emerging Trends in Real Estate 2016* survey.

Note: Based on U.S. respondents only.

adds to relatively fixed inventory, is faced with a potential reduction in demand.

Some of our interviewees feel that is exactly the Airbnb challenge, and it is directed upscale. A sophisticated capital manager expressed it this way: "I personally know people who are booking though Airbnb with their families instead of staying at four- or five-star hotels. In fact, on a percentage basis, it might be more impactful because there are fewer of them. People who would have normally gone to a Four Seasons are looking at Airbnb."

She continued, saying, "Someone was telling me that their cousin bought houses in the Boston area to make available for these types of services for travelers. So [the cousin] has bought them for investment purposes and [is] renting them out on these services via Airbnb and Home Away. That's a real phenomenon."

Boutique hotels also are competing to take market share from established chains, intensifying a trend we identified last year. "Everyone is trying to stay ahead with design forward," noted one hotel investor, who also indicated strong demand dynamics in 18-hour markets like Nashville and Austin. In New York, the avatar of the 24-hour city, hotel supply is up, but occupancies have not declined, thanks to the annual tourist flow of 54 million visitors there. Room rates were said to be flat in the Big Apple, but that is flat at a stratospheric level for many guests. One private equity player said, "Smart investors are starting to sell NYC hotels. That's a sign."

Could the cycle have topped out for hotels? Perhaps. It is very much a cyclical industry, and getting more complicated over time. No wonder the trend is for capital to align with operators who can provide "alpha" opportunities, with institutional and cross-border investors supplementing that with purchases like Manhattan's Waldorf Astoria, a proven asset retaining its value decade after decade.

Retail

Fluidity as well as granularity are the forces shaping retail property trends going forward. Stripped down to essentials, the key is "how do you get goods to the customer?" An analyst specializing in this sector sees the conversion of function in retailing—namely, on-floor selling to order fulfillment—as a dynamic characterized by stores shifting from "showrooms" to "web rooms" to "guide rooms." The major mall operators are bringing think-tanks (a.k.a, "skunk works") to their management procedures. Staying ahead of the game *is* the game.

In retrospect, it is unlikely that many will credit the 2011 Occupy Wall Street demonstrations as having much lasting effect on the economy. It is certain, though, that the sloganeering about the 1 percent and the 99 percent has altered the framework of economic discourse. Income inequality is front and center in the national discussion, like it or not. A May 2015 Gallup poll shows 63 percent of American adults agreeing that the national income distribution is unfair, a position that is endorsed by 42 percent of self-described conservatives.

Why would this be germane to a discussion of real estate prospects? If you are in retailing, you know the answer all too well. Knowledgeable investors and developers focused on shopping centers speak about the "barbell" in retailing: success in "value" retailing and in the luxury segment, while stores catering to the middle of the income distribution struggle year after year. Job gains are noted, but they do not translate into improved revenues at the merchants unless accompanied by wage growth.

Much depends upon the future of income growth in the lagging sectors. That is why the income inequality issue is vitally relevant for merchants and for shopping center investors. That is especially true for centers designed for the shrinking number of middle-class households. One investment manager sees a tremendous number of "dead malls" to be dealt with over the next few years. A major financing firm sifts the sands this way: "In the Midwest, the best retail locations have largely bounced back, but B and B-minus centers are overbuilt and need to be redeployed." A Chicago-based builder/owner looked at his home metro area and said, "Suburbs are a wasteland around Chicago. Schaumberg and Naperville are dying for dollars."

As Pew Research data show, over the past three decades wealth for middle-income households has hardly moved the needle, while upper-income household wealth has doubled, in real dollar terms.

It is impossible to accurately analyze the outlook for the retail property sector if such data are not factored in. "High-end retail will prosper as the high-end population does well; commodity [or mass-market] retail will suffer," predicts a top analyst we interviewed. An asset manager observes, "Retail is in flux. A small number of really top malls are going to do well, but after that it is tricky. . . . It will take some time to sort out."

NCREIF's data for retail look excellent, for example. A longtime monitor of institutional trends says, "Retail is still a top performer [for this class of investor] in spite of all the negative talk." Retail assets have turned in the highest total returns of all property types in two of the last three years, and also lead the long-term performance measures of the ten- and 20-year time horizons.

Yet, according to the first-quarter 2015 NCREIF discussion of its retail index, "lackluster retail sales growth, limited new store openings and continued store closures, and an overhang of crippled retail centers" burden the shopping center picture. Nevertheless, the NCREIF data's focus on "higher quality, more institutional properties . . . insulates it from these trends." Meanwhile, those centers in the bottom third of trade area demographics languish.

The upshot is that both demand and supply in the retail sector have lagged behind their long-run averages in this recovery, and are projected to remain sub-par a while longer (exhibit 4-18). While investment prices for retail assets have risen 62

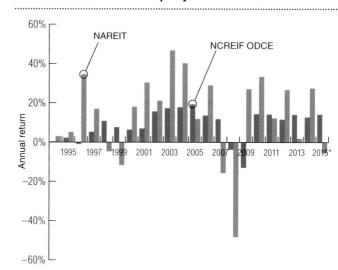

Exhibit 4-17 U.S. Retail Property Total Returns

Sources: NCREIF Fund Index Open-End Diversified Core (ODCE); NAREIT Equity REIT Index.
* Returns as of June 30, 2015.

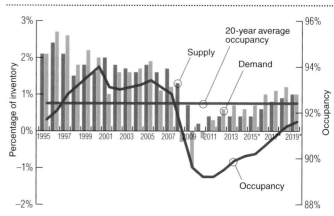

Exhibit 4-18 Change in Supply and Demand—U.S. Retail

Source: REIS Inc.
* Forecast.

percent since the trough of the Great Recession, they are still 7.5 percent below their prior peak (exhibit 4-2). The situation in a half-dozen major markets is the exception, as these urban areas have seen prices move 4.1 percent above pre–global financial crisis levels.

Generally speaking, transaction volume for retail has been rising annually throughout the present decade, and hit $91.3 billion for the 12 months ending June 2015. A large private equity investor reflects, "I thought retail was really quiet after the recession.

Exhibit 4-19 Retail Investment Prospect Trends

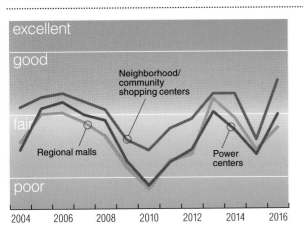

excellent

good

Neighborhood/
community
shopping centers

fair

Regional malls

Power
centers

poor

2004   2006   2008   2010   2012   2014   2016

Source: *Emerging Trends in Real Estate* surveys.

U.S. neighborhood/community shopping centers

2016	Prospects	Ranking
Investment prospects	3.54	7
Development prospects	3.35	10

Buy 37.5%	Hold 41.1%	Sell 21.4%

Expected capitalization rate, December 2016	6.3%

U.S. power centers

2016	Prospects	Ranking
Investment prospects	3.00	15
Development prospects	2.61	15

Buy 9.9%	Hold 41.0%	Sell 49.1%

Expected capitalization rate, December 2016	6.5%

U.S. regional malls

2016	Prospects	Ranking
Investment prospects	2.79	16
Development prospects	2.04	16

Buy 9.3%	Hold 44.2%	Sell 46.5%

Expected capitalization rate, December 2016	6.0%

Source: *Emerging Trends in Real Estate 2016* survey.
Note: Based on U.S. respondents only.

In the past year and a half, it seems to be picking up. National players are looking to do deals in this market." Capital trends discussed in chapter 2 give every indication that retail property investment activity will again be brisk in 2016. As one experienced investor said in her interview, **"What we've gotten right**

about the retail sector is that it is subject to disruption. What we've gotten wrong is the expectation that everything will shift. It turns out that stores are a very effective delivery system."

Urban/high street. When two high-end department stores elect to put new flagship stores in Manhattan, while eschewing regional mall opportunities elsewhere in the metropolitan area, that's news. And at the same time, the nation's largest chain of department stores has announced a development deal featuring the renovation of a venerable downtown Brooklyn facility, redesigning 310,000 square feet as contemporary retail space while converting some upper floors into headquarters-quality office space. That's more news. Ireland's largest retailer purchases an iconic former department store at Boston's Downtown Crossing. Still more news. Keep it up, and we'll see a trend!

A REIT executive predicts, "Main Street retail will outperform other offerings. This fits with the migration of population into urban environments." At some level, that's undeniable, though the caveat of a pension fund investor should be acknowledged: "I wouldn't turn down a deal if there's a specific value proposition . . . more a rifle shot than a scattered-shot approach."

A veteran mall developer, looking at center city retail opportunities, argues, "It depends on the neighborhood. Retailers are choosy about which area of the city they are going. Different neighborhoods dictate different uses in the retail project." Still, there can be surprises. One investor has a deal in the south Bronx where he saw beyond its 1970s reputation and found a high-volume transportation hub and great population density, with local employment generators including a college, the county courts, and a major hospital. Spots supporting high-rise multifamily development and investment—think South Lake Union in Seattle, Bunker Hill in Los Angeles, Fountain Square in Cincinnati—fit the description of the kind of walkable, amenity-laden neighborhoods that support high street retailing.

Neighborhood/community centers. *Emerging Trends* survey respondents concluded "good" investment prospects for smaller shopping centers in 2016, according them the best outlook score in the past dozen years (exhibit 4-19). On the buy/hold/sell decision, such centers are favored as a "buy" by 37.5 percent of our sample, versus just 21.4 percent making "sell" recommendations. This is in line with the empirical evidence showing increasing transaction volume and falling capitalization rates for such assets.

A Midwest developer sees these smaller shopping centers experiencing a shift in tenant mix. "Grocery store wars are in full swing," he remarks, "with a push toward 'organics'-branded stores needing facilities of 20,000 to 25,000 square feet." Also in this niche we find value merchandisers backfilling locations in tightly defined trade areas. NCREIF investors already have $26.4 billion invested in neighborhood and community shopping centers, and they have been posting annual returns averaging more than 12 percent for the past five years.

While the demographic mix in the United States changes, so does its retail mix. Hispanic-themed centers are springing up as one-sixth of the U.S. population identifies as Latino, and we should expect other immigrant groups to claim their share of store area. Most major cities have long had Asian ethnic enclaves, which had significant urban retail components. As the newer wave of Asian immigration surpasses the Hispanic cohort in its growth rate (now nearly 3 percent per annum for Asians), and the retailing community recognizes this population segment as older, better educated, and more affluent than other immigrant groups, shopping opportunities targeted to them should be an emerging development/redevelopment theme in the years ahead.

Malls. Love 'em or hate 'em, "Mall companies are doing great," said one developer with experience across the United States in several property types. The head of a capital management firm calls it "a tale of two strategies: the first is the demalling of America, where the second-best mall in a trade area may not survive; but a focus on the very top tier can be very rewarding."

Institutional returns on the top tier have surpassed the performance measures of the smaller shopping centers by a considerable margin. Regional malls have average annual total returns of 14.2 percent, and super-regional malls' returns have been even higher at 16.0 percent. That is enough to keep attracting capital. There's a limit to new competition, too, as the prime sites have long since been developed and the regulatory hurdles to development have only gotten more challenging since the last generation of mall building. Cap rates for malls are a pricey 5.9 percent, and even lower in the Northeast and on the West Coast.

Technology, e-commerce, and multichannel retailing. Now that the obvious has long since been stated, "Shopping online will make retail space dwindle," it is time to see how the details of this trend will be working out. The "bricks and clicks" discussion is going to get sharper, and in a hurry. Stores have punched back, adopting e-commerce for their own operations and, as we noted last year, internet retailers have increasingly been dabbling in physical stores as a supplement to online sales.

That is getting more common, and both sides are converging in multichannel customer access.

The application of technology is a much larger issue, and a much bigger operational trend than merely e-commerce. Technology now lets a mall see that you are approaching the center (or maybe passing it by) and can beam out a message or coupon that is not only an ad, but, depending on your social media profile, also an invitation tailored to your preferences. A goal, said one interviewee, is "to make your in-store experience more like being online." We are really going down the rabbit hole here!

Tenant mix continues to evolve. What is not replaceable by the internet is moving to the fore. "Restaurants and food are key. Market halls, the 21st-century version of a food court, are now very popular," in the words of one major developer. "Food is the password for many millennials and boomers alike. They both spend a lot of their disposable income on food. Food culture is a growing trend. Chefs are now celebrities in many cities like Minneapolis and Louisville. Brew pubs are also a growing phenomenon. They are being incorporated into malls as well."

A top retail broker mused, "The selfie generation is all foodies, too. Look at the cell phone pictures being snapped every night in restaurants and posted on Instagram."

It's not just food, of course, but personal services, too (massage, dental, yoga studios, fitness centers), and entertainment. It's all lifestyle oriented.

It is becoming more obvious to the investment community that online retailers, even the biggest ones, have not been making money for their shareholders in the form of cash profits, only in increasing stock prices. And this has been in an era when many were below the sales-tax radar. One savvy player puts it this way: "One of the reasons why online sales grow so fast is that they are so cheap. They don't cover their costs. Stock investors know this about the profit picture, but think, 'We'll get there.' At some point, like every other industry, they will have to make money from operations." A marketing specialist declares even more forcefully, "The music is stopping for pure play in e-commerce. Stores are the new black."

That may overstate the case. Surely, the commodity retailers who have nearly vanished from sales of music, books, travel, and the like are probably never coming back. But the penetration of the bricks domain with the clicks is only at the early stage of maturation. That evolution is the emerging trend—and it has its limits. One astute observer made this argument about e-commerce growth: "Going from 1 percent to 2 percent market share is easy. Five percent to 10 percent is harder. Ten percent to 20 percent is not likely to happen."

The e-commerce share is just about at the 9 percent mark as of right now.

Housing

Residential starts came in at 1.2 million for the months of June and July 2015, the best construction activity for housing since late 2007. More telling, the growth was spurred by single-family housing after apartment development had provided the momentum during the past several years. The elements of a housing development trend toward greater normalcy are falling into place, after the catastrophic bursting of the mortgage-induced bubble of a decade ago.

The inventory of finished new homes for sale is 5.4 months, right in line with historical averages, and price increases are beginning to reflect scarcity on the supply side. This condition sets the stage for further gains in 2016, since there is a shortage of ready-to-build housing lots. Banks' skittishness about land and development loans—a major source of losses during the financial crisis—has meant that builders have not been able to get the pipeline for production anywhere near historical capacity.

The CEO of a private equity firm focused on land development picks housing as a "best bet" over the next three years. "Residential, residential, residential. Single-family, multifamily, and single-family to be rented. It's a safe bet that you will outstrip inflation by a couple of percent by doing that. You will get above-normal historical returns by doing residential, all three legs of the stool."

Housing and the economy. A virtuous feedback loop exists between housing development and housing demand. It obviously can be disrupted by excess, as it has in the past, but right now that feedback is strengthening. The link is construction jobs. The renewal of homebuilding is shifting employment trends in ways not visible in top-line national statistics. Construction employment growth has been tepid, although it has risen in 32 of the past 36 months. But government funding of infrastructure projects, or the inadequacy thereof, has been a drag on the numbers. Homebuilding, which is labor-intensive, is the counterbalance, especially in an era of disciplined commercial development.

The multiplier effect of housing growth carries over into all sorts of other jobs in the building supplies industry, in furniture and appliances, and in wholesale and retail trade. The low interest

Exhibit 4-20 Prospects for Residential Property Types in 2016

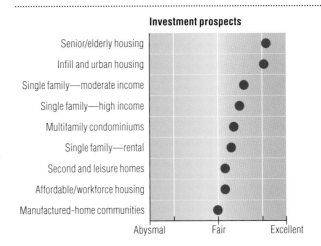

Investment prospects

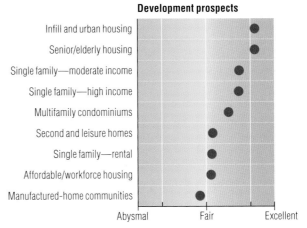

Development prospects

Source: *Emerging Trends in Real Estate 2016* survey.

Note: Based on U.S. respondents only.

rate policies of the Fed have kept 30-year fixed-rate mortgages under 4 percent, and while rates will be trending upward they will still be at stimulative levels if the expected path of policy change is executed—gradual and moderate increases, taking care not to shock the recovery. That should buttress more than homebuilding itself.

Single-family-for-rent investors. During the dark days of the global financial crisis, some forward thinkers moved into the housing breach, anticipating a "flip" over time, when renters-by-necessity would become buyers-by-choice. That thinking is changing somewhat, and one banker likes single-family rentals as the logical way to understand a reduced homeownership rate and the viability of suburbs. Her view has generation Y thinking, "I want to move to the suburbs, but I still want to rent because I still need flexibility." So we are seeing single-family home rentals evolving from the "flip" strategy to becoming operating businesses.

One lender has a different perspective, linking such investments to housing affordability. "It's a challenging market, it's complicated from a regulatory point of view, even from an investment point of view. There's such an incredible need. We actually think **one of the ways the affordable housing stock can be increased efficiently and effectively is through the support of the new single-family rental companies, looking at that as an emerging industry.** Those companies own single-family houses, they maintain them, and they rent them out [with] a pretty big chunk as affordable housing. They're not just a bunch of mansions that were overbuilt. I think it's starting to work. I think it's going to come into its own in the next 18 months; it's really an emerging industry."

Master-planned communities. Affording an opportunity to target the live/work/play sweet spot very directly, master-planned communities have risen to the third position in the rankings of niche investment and development prospects for 2016, up from eighth place (for investment) and sixth place (for development) a year ago. Most often located in suburban locations, such communities are increasingly taking on urban forms. This is partly a result of the "new urbanism" concepts evolving over the past 20 years, and partly a response to millennials' preferences. So we see greater pedestrianization, integration of retailing and amenities (including parks and schools) with housing in community design, community gardens concepts, and aspects of the "sharing economy" in transportation and coworking spaces. Intergenerational living is a factor, too. This is a kind of back-to-the-future element, partly reflective of active seniors' lifestyle, partly a recognition of the "boomerang" phenomenon among generation Y, and partly a recognition that diversity of age is a desirable feature for any sustainable community.

Niche products. For certain investors, niche products like student housing and senior housing are maintaining momentum as attractive choices. This is an example of a trend previously identified that is working its way forward. Fund managers are reporting increased interest from capital providers, both domestic and international, for exposure to these products.

Demographics obviously counts for a lot in student and senior housing, but again our interviewees stress the importance of nuance and granularity in evaluating opportunities. One investor active in both niches says, "Housing investment is steady at 'good' or 'flagship' schools, but there are enrollment issues at

lesser-known public universities and private schools. Over time, we are watching demand shifts: there will be less of the population in that age group—the 18-year-old population peaked four to five years ago." And, obviously, student housing is operationally intensive. It needs great hands-on management, not just passive investors, to succeed.

The baby boomers have long been anticipated as a huge market for a cafeteria menu of senior housing choices. But as in so many other instances, this generation has confounded expectations. Right now, in early retirement (or deferring retirement), boomers are more likely to be empty nesters than seeking their long-range housing solution. But that will be coming. And so, this year, housing for seniors ranks first for investment in the *Emerging Trends 2016* survey (exhibit 4-20).

An executive in a health care REIT with significant seniors' housing experience had the following to say: "Today, the average age of someone in senior housing is about 85. That's up significantly and continues to increase. You see people live longer, with higher acuity. It's still a lifestyle choice, but it's a lifestyle choice because of need. People are selling their home to pick a different lifestyle choice. It's like going back to apartment living, except that you've got food, entertainment, people so that you don't have to be lonely, and people who will be there if you need help."

True enough, but the oldest baby boomer is still under 70 years of age right now. We can glimpse the future opportunity—and still recognize execution issues for now. Selling the existing home is, for now, not a "given." Shortfalls in savings are a problem for many households: fewer than half of U.S. households have retirement accounts. Those who are near retirement age and have such accounts have a median balance of only $104,000, according to a 2015 study conducted by the National Institute of Retirement Security; those without such accounts have median savings of just $14,500. In light of such economics, senior housing is like so many other investment segments in requiring careful scrutiny and very targeted selection.

Emerging Trends in Canada

"It's a time of transition for the Canadian real estate markets, but it's not a time for pessimism. Across the country, opportunities abound—only they're not necessarily the same ones that have driven the markets' growth in recent years."

The story of Canadian real estate this year is one of shifting economic fortunes and changing real estate trends. The decline in oil prices has caused a sharp slowdown in the Calgary and Edmonton economies, and the long-term impact on the local real estate markets remains to be seen. At the time of writing, the Canadian economy has had a second quarter of minor decline—largely a result of the impact of oil in Alberta. Yet these low energy prices—and the low Canadian dollar—are improving the prospects for manufacturing, transportation, warehousing, and other sectors across the country, especially in eastern Canada. As economic power returns to the east, investors and developers are turning their attention to new opportunities in faster-growing Toronto and some parts of Montreal. Vancouver is the exception in the west, as it retains the top real estate investment spot.

This year's top-ranked property subsectors reflect the changing nature of Canada's real estate market. Warehouses, fulfillment centers, and neighborhood shopping centers are among the top-ranked this year. Each is a classic defensive play in times of slower economic growth, and even minor negative economic growth—yet each of these sectors is also ideally positioned to capitalize on periods of stable domestic consumer demand and increased exports, especially to the United States. In our view, to interpret this as a sign of firms "battening down the hatches" in preparation for an economic storm would be to miss the larger point—which is that opportunities are changing, but they still exist.

We see other signs of real estate players responding positively to changes in their markets and identifying new growth opportunities. Investor interest in medical office and health care properties is perking up as an aging baby boomer generation makes increasing demands on the health care sector. As the rise in housing prices continues to outpace Canadians' income growth, especially in markets like Toronto and Vancouver, more

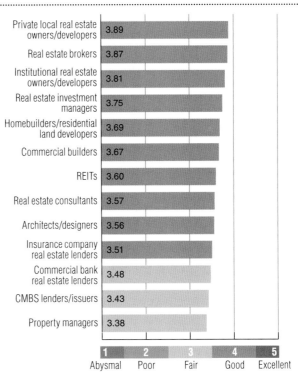

Exhibit 5-1 Real Estate Business Prospects for 2016

Private local real estate owners/developers	3.89
Real estate brokers	3.87
Institutional real estate owners/developers	3.81
Real estate investment managers	3.75
Homebuilders/residential land developers	3.69
Commercial builders	3.67
REITs	3.60
Real estate consultants	3.57
Architects/designers	3.56
Insurance company real estate lenders	3.51
Commercial bank real estate lenders	3.48
CMBS lenders/issuers	3.43
Property managers	3.38

1 Abysmal 2 Poor 3 Fair 4 Good 5 Excellent

Source: *Emerging Trends in Real Estate 2016* survey.
Note: Based on Canadian investors only.

and more people are choosing to rent—permanently, in some cases. Even some retirees are opting to rent after they sell their homes, rather than buy a smaller home. Developers are keen to meet this growing demand with new purpose-built rental units. However, some of our interviewees expressed concern with the number of purpose-built rental projects announced in Toronto, citing concerns with whether the numbers really do work yet.

Exhibit 5-2 2016 Forecast Economic Indicators

	Real GDP growth (%)	Total employment growth (%)	Unemployment rate (%)	Personal income per capita growth (%)	Population growth (%)	Total housing starts	Retail sales growth (%)
Vancouver	3.2	2.1	5.6	3.1	1.7	20,500	4.8
Toronto	3.2	2.5	7.1	3.0	1.9	33,095	4.1
Winnipeg	3.0	2.1	5.2	3.0	1.3	3,946	4.0
Halifax	2.8	2.0	5.7	3.1	1.1	1,841	4.4
Montreal	2.7	1.9	7.6	3.3	1.1	16,595	4.0
Saskatoon	2.2	1.0	4.7	0.8	2.4	3,114	2.8
Ottawa	2.1	1.9	6.2	3.2	1.0	7,241	3.8
Calgary	1.5	1.3	6.2	1.8	1.9	11,010	2.5
Edmonton	1.3	1.2	5.1	1.8	1.8	11,590	2.4

Source: Conference Board of Canada, *Metropolitan Outlook 1: Economic Insights into 13 Canadian Metropolitan Economies*, Spring 2015.

Exhibit 5-3 Emerging Trends Barometer 2016

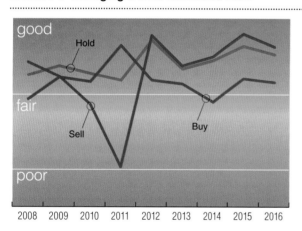

Source: *Emerging Trends in Real Estate 2016* survey.

Note: Based on Canadian investors only.

Mixed-use developments with residential and retail real estate space have also grown beyond a trend and have become a requirement in and around Toronto and Vancouver.

Caution and prudence characterize today's Canadian real estate players. Many of our survey respondents suspect that Canada's real estate markets are due for a breather after seven-plus years of expansion, and they are acting accordingly. Some are slowing their acquisition efforts in Canada, and focusing their attention on existing holdings and opportunities in the United States and other foreign markets. Landlords are concentrating on bringing in new tenants—and extending the leases of existing ones. In Calgary, industry players are settling into a holding pattern as they wait out the current downturn, avoiding rash action.

Calgary and Edmonton—and, to a lesser extent, Saskatoon—aside, the outlook for Canadian real estate remains generally stable. Condominium sales remain solid, and single-family homes continue to do well despite affordability worries. The boom in office construction in recent years is giving rise to some oversupply concerns, at least in the near term. And industrial property across much of the country is poised for growth in the current export-friendly environment.

Without a doubt, Canada's real estate market is undergoing important shifts—but it would be wrong to take a pessimistic view of the current environment. Opportunities may be changing, but Canadian real estate players should remain confident that good opportunities exist across the country.

Emerging Trends in Canadian Real Estate

"The real estate market in Canada has nine lives. Every time a correction should have happened, something else goes wrong locally or worldwide and causes a distraction."

Caution Rules as Firms Position Themselves for the Next Business Cycle

How long can Canada's real estate market continue to grow? It's a question many in the industry are asking these days. The Canadian economy and real estate market have grown consistently or stayed stable in the seven years since the global economic downturn, and the 13 years leading up to it. Some respondents suspect a downturn is coming—sooner rather than later.

It's a line of thinking that is convincing real estate companies to adopt a more prudent, defensive position. With competition

Exhibit 5-4 **Forecast Net Migration, 2015–2019**

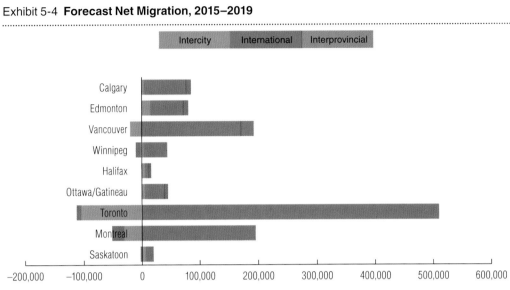

Source: Conference Board of Canada.

Exhibit 5-5 **Real Estate Capital Market Balance Forecast**

Equity capital for investing

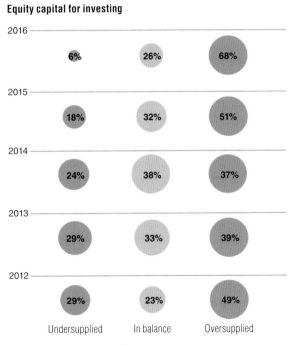

Source: *Emerging Trends in Real Estate* surveys.
Note: Based on Canadian investors only.

for high-quality properties intensifying, large real estate players are slowing their pace of acquisitions in Canada; while they opt to wait and see where the Canadian market is heading, they are looking to the United States and elsewhere for opportuni-

ties. Some companies, including real estate investment trusts (REITs), are culling noncore property holdings to capitalize on high valuations and raise capital for redevelopment or intensification projects. Landlords are working to sign tenants to longer-term leases. And most companies are taking the long view when it comes to their business strategy.

However, this heightened level of caution appears to be driven by pragmatism, not pessimism. True, respondents are concerned about the impact of low energy prices on western Canada's markets. While many feel that U.S. and European economic performance is less than ideal, others see opportunities in those markets as well as in South America. Few seem to believe that these wider economic factors will cause significant problems for their business. More than anything else, it seems that respondents believe that the Canadian market is due for a breather.

Liquidity Everywhere, but Nothing to Buy

While there's a lot of liquidity in the Canadian market, there isn't much to invest it in. Respondents talk about the severe lack of high-quality product available for purchase right now, given the current cost of capital. Prized, top-tier Canadian properties are increasingly in the hands of pension funds, institutional investors, and REITs, which in some cases are selling their Tier 2 assets to help fund the purchases. As a result, transaction volumes have picked up for secondary assets and value-added plays. While this creates a steady supply of product, respondents point out that the properties often are older and require investment to suit current market needs.

Exhibit 5-6 Real Estate Capital Market Balance Forecast

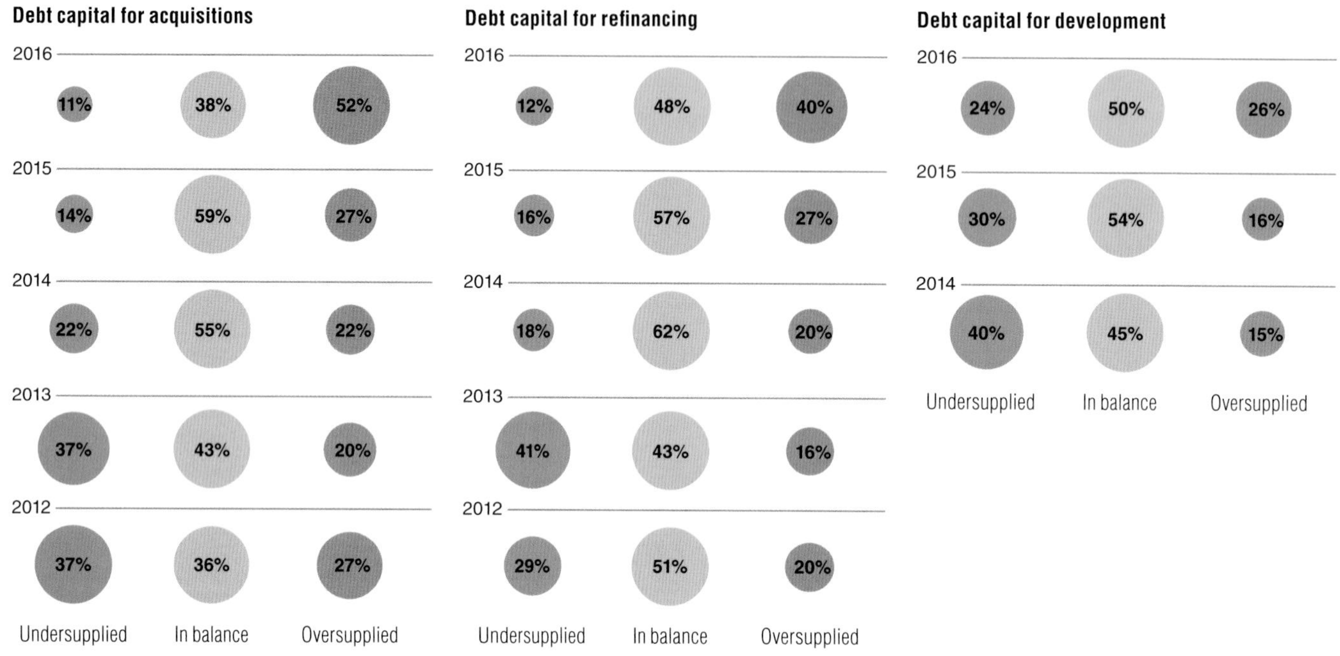

Debt capital for acquisitions

2016		
11%	38%	52%

2015		
14%	59%	27%

2014		
22%	55%	22%

2013		
37%	43%	20%

2012		
37%	36%	27%

| Undersupplied | In balance | Oversupplied |

Debt capital for refinancing

2016		
12%	48%	40%

2015		
16%	57%	27%

2014		
18%	62%	20%

2013		
41%	43%	16%

2012		
29%	51%	20%

| Undersupplied | In balance | Oversupplied |

Debt capital for development

2016		
24%	50%	26%

2015		
30%	54%	16%

2014		
40%	45%	15%

| Undersupplied | In balance | Oversupplied |

Source: *Emerging Trends in Real Estate* surveys.
Note: Based on Canadian investors only.

Office Leasing: Yield Is King, but the Rules Are Changing

"The workplace has to be viewed as a stimulus to productivity."

With so little top-tier product available, respondents are maximizing their existing holdings. Yield is king, and companies are focused on attracting new tenants to existing office properties—and extending the leases of existing tenants—in order to generate stable income.

Yet respondents say that leasing itself is changing, in part as a response to tenants' own business challenges. Instead of ten- to 15-year leases, respondents say that tenants want leases of ten years or less. Tenants are also reducing space per employee, and some tenants are sharing offices, or opting for value over high-end, luxury amenities. Respondents report that it is becoming increasingly critical to engage the tenants' human resources groups and others in organizations to secure new leasing. Some tenants are declining traditional property management services like cleaning, choosing to engage their own, often less costly, suppliers.

Stronger U.S. Dollar a Source of Mild Optimism

Economic uncertainties in China and Europe have Canadian firms once again looking to the United States to drive growth.

It's not without risk, of course: the U.S. recovery is not especially strong, and many U.S. trading partners are not growing.

The U.S. dollar's relative strength could well benefit Canadian real estate markets, particularly in eastern Canada. Respondents believe that Toronto-area industrial development, especially distribution centers, may be boosted by the U.S. dollar. Should U.S. firms choose to capitalize on the stronger U.S. dollar to hire skilled Canadian staff, the office sector, especially suburban office properties located near or on transportation hubs, may also benefit.

Lower Oil Prices Have Mixed Impact on Canadian Real Estate

The sharp drop in oil prices has led some to speculate that eastern Canada will regain its position as Canada's economic engine. However, the impact of the energy sector downturn on Canadian real estate—in Alberta and elsewhere—has yet to be fully felt.

Oxford Economics' May 2015 report, *Canada: The Negative Impact of Lower Oil Prices*, forecast a 20 percent drop in energy sector investment this year, and indeed Canadian energy companies have postponed or shelved many projects in light

Exhibit 5-7 Foreign Direct Investment in Canada

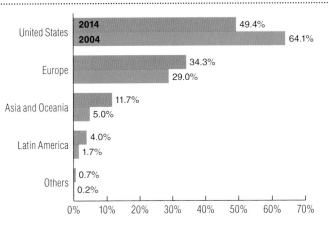

Source: Statistics Canada, April 2015.

Exhibit 5-8 Housing Affordability

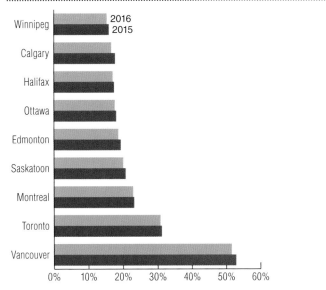

Mortgage payment as % of average household income

Source: TD Economics, *Quarterly Regional Housing Report*, February 12, 2015.

Note: Mortgage payment is based on the average home price, 25 percent downpayment, 25-year amortization, and five-year fixed posted rate.

of business conditions. Yet on the real estate side, investors appear to be biding their time. There are little to no real estate purchases or sales taking place in Alberta, although firms are putting space up for sublet. Alberta's experience with boom-and-bust cycles has taught companies that sometimes the best strategy is to simply hold.

Elsewhere, low energy prices may prove a boon to certain sectors and their related real estate markets. Canada's weaker currency should make the country's nonenergy exports more competitive. If gas pump savings should materialize, this too could boost business and consumer spending, potentially benefiting retailers, among others. This could, in turn, drive activity in industrial, office, and commercial real estate, especially in the east.

Foreign Investment: Canada Retains Its Allure

"There will always be one guy who needs it more than someone else."

Global investors continue to see Canada as a safe haven for their capital, and the lower Canadian dollar only adds to the allure. Many respondents expect foreign investment to continue to flow into Canadian real estate—not only into traditional markets like Vancouver, Calgary, and Toronto, but also into Montreal and even Saskatchewan, where interest in farmland and development land is rising.

Foreign investors face numerous hurdles in entering the Canadian market. As a result, they are determined to ensure that they realize a good return on their investments. Interest in hotel and office properties is rising, and observers expect that foreign

investors will soon turn to Canadian health care real estate, especially as the U.S. health care real estate market matures.

However, like their institutional counterparts, foreign investors are also finding that premium opportunities are expensive and in short supply, and it remains to be seen whether this will cool their interest in the Canadian market. It is equally unclear what impact the slowdown in Canada's energy sector will have on foreign investment.

Housing Affordability Concerns on the Rise

While developers are building condominiums and mid-density products like stacked townhouses to meet municipal and provincial urban density demands, it is getting harder for developers to build affordable housing in the urban centers that people covet—which could have consequences for Canada's urbanization trend.

Developers and builders believe that several issues are pushing housing prices up and potentially out of reach for many prospective homebuyers. Land prices continue to rise, and many believe that provincial government policies are a key factor: greenbelt legislation in Ontario and British Columbia, for example, is limiting land supplies in an effort to promote urban densification. In addition, lengthy approval processes and significant development charges also are limiting supply and driving up costs across the

Exhibit 5-9 Average Home Prices and Price to Income Ratio*

	2013 Price	Price to income ratio	2014 Price	Price to income ratio	2015 Price	Price to income ratio	2016 Price	Price to income ratio
Vancouver	$767,400	10.4 : 1	$813,200	10.8 : 1	$889,100	11.6 : 1	$921,900	11.6 : 1
Edmonton	$343,600	4.3 : 1	$361,300	4.4 : 1	$366,700	4.3 : 1	$357,100	4.3 : 1
Calgary	$436,600	4.0 : 1	$459,500	4.0 : 1	$451,300	3.9 : 1	$441,700	3.9 : 1
Saskatoon	$287,500	4.6 : 1	$297,900	4.6 : 1	$297,800	4.5 : 1	$297,800	4.5 : 1
Winnipeg	$268,500	3.7 : 1	$271,900	3.5 : 1	$275,200	3.5 : 1	$279,200	3.5 : 1
Toronto	$521,800	6.3 : 1	$563,500	6.6 : 1	$614,400	7.0 : 1	$639,300	7.0 : 1
Ottawa	$356,400	4.0 : 1	$360,700	3.9 : 1	$368,300	3.9 : 1	$375,400	3.9 : 1
Montreal	$324,100	5.1 : 1	$331,800	5.1 : 1	$336,800	5.0 : 1	$344,000	5.0 : 1
Halifax	$274,200	3.9 : 1	$275,300	3.8 : 1	$279,200	3.8 : 1	$285,200	3.8 : 1
Canada	$381,700	5.3 : 1	$407,000	5.5 : 1	$435,800	5.7 : 1	$440,100	5.7 : 1

* The "price to income ratio" is the ratio of the metro-area average home price to the median income.

Source: TD Economics, *Canadian Regional Housing Outlook*, August 2015.

country. And then there are the construction costs themselves, which continue to rise.

Affordability issues could potentially change urbanization trends, some argue. One respondent sees homeowners selling their homes, moving further out from the core to a less expensive house, and banking the remaining equity. Expansion of the regional transit systems across major urban areas may make it easier for people to buy more affordable homes further out from the core; one respondent remarked that self-driving automobiles could have a similar impact, by making lengthy commutes less of a burden. The longer-term impact on development in the core, however, remains to be seen.

Of course, a rise in interest rates could make housing even less affordable than it is currently and drive more significant changes in real estate markets. That said, the current combination of low oil prices, low mortgage rates, and ample housing supplies could slightly improve affordability, at least in the near term (see exhibit 5-8).

Rise of the Renters

"There is a trend in rentals that will emerge over time: people will want to rent luxury—by choice, not because they can't afford to buy."

As concerns over housing affordability grow, a rising number of Canadian households are choosing to rent rather than buy. It's a trend that is expected to continue and create new opportunities across the country.

Exhibit 5-10 Rapid Transit Infrastructure Underway

	Length of rapid transit lines (km)	Total investment (C$ billion)
Toronto	59.2	C$14.00
Montreal	14.0	C$0.42
Vancouver	11.0	C$1.55
Calgary	25.0	C$0.80
Ottawa	12.5	C$2.13

Source: Pembina Institute, *Fast Cities: A Comparison of Rapid Transit in Major Canadian Cities*, September 5, 2014.

Notes: Figures are for instrastructure funded or under construction. Investment is in 2014 dollars.

Attitudes about renting have changed, respondents note. Renting is no longer seen only as a temporary step on the road to homeownership, but as an alternative. Today, we are seeing the rise of permanent renters—a new demographic in the Canadian market, especially as a growing proportion of the population cannot assemble the downpayment for a new home. This is not new in Montreal, but is relatively new in other cities. Changes to lending rules, which have effectively doubled minimum downpayments, have not helped, and rising house prices just add to the challenge. Faced with a choice between long commutes from suburbs or renting in the urban core, more and more people are opting to rent.

But that is not the only reason that renting is on the rise. Some older homeowners are often opting to sell their homes and cash out, moving into high-end or luxury rental units and keeping the

Exhibit 5-11 Prime Multifamily Rental Units, by Year of Construction

	Total	Before 1960	1960–1979	1980–1999	2000 or later
Quebec	791,402	325,587	291,429	120,355	54,031
Ontario	664,519	134,536	431,368	71,659	26,956
British Columbia	176,746	24,460	112,415	28,152	11,719
Alberta	132,428	7,634	84,610	25,414	14,770
Manitoba	62,894	13,150	35,427	7,735	6,582
Nova Scotia	52,619	7,603	20,608	13,576	11,372
Saskatchewan	34,797	4,372	20,412	7,325	2,688
New Brunswick	32,307	7,942	11,327	6,038	7,000
Prince Edward Island	6,485	1,465	1,025	2,289	1,716
Newfoundland/Labrador	5,720	1,224	2,720	1,233	543
Canada total	**1,961,877**	**527,986**	**1,011,494**	**284,544**	**137,853**

Source: Canadian Mortgage and Housing Corporation, "Rental Market Survey," 2015.

Exhibit 5-12 Prospects for Commercial/Multifamily Subsectors in 2016

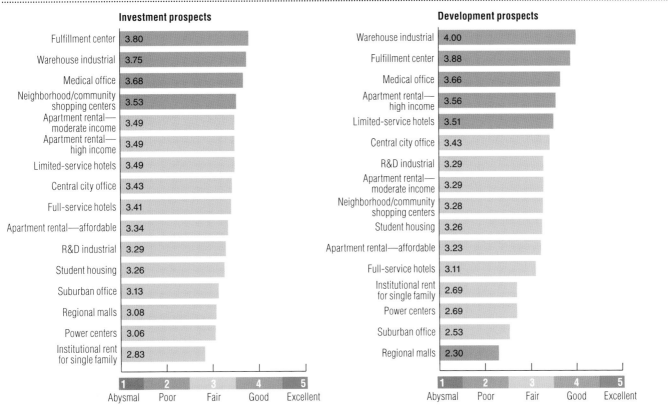

Source: *Emerging Trends in Real Estate 2016* survey.

Note: Based on Canadian investors only.

proceeds from the sale for spending. Luxury apartment units aimed at baby boomers and retirees could be increasingly popular in the years to come, noted one respondent. Offering flexibility, high quality, and low maintenance, rented luxury units will provide a comfortable bridge between homeownership and retirement homes.

With housing affordability likely to remain an issue for some time, rentals are expected to continue to be in demand. These properties offer investors steady income and stable cash flows; in the current environment, that is an attractive proposition. Respondents expect to see more condos redeveloped into rental properties; they also expect to see more purpose-built multiunit rentals come on stream, since the current, aging stock of multiunit residential is not well suited to the demand for high-quality rental units. Further cap-rate compression for multiresidential product in eastern Canada is making a compelling case to build rather than buy. Some observers, however, have raised concerns about new players entering the multiresidential market and competing with established players; multiresidential is a unique segment, and new players may find themselves facing greater-than-expected challenges.

Alternative Property Types and Secondary Markets

With intense competition for top-tier properties limiting opportunities and putting pressure on yields, investors are searching the market for overlooked or underserved niches. Shifting demographic and economic trends are driving interest in a number of alternative property types.

Health Care Real Estate

"Health care as a real estate class is becoming more accepted globally, and more dollars are being invested in health care real estate entities."

Investors are starting to pay much more attention to medical office and health care real estate opportunities as aging, health-conscious baby boomers begin to fuel a sharp rise in demand for health care services. While U.S. investors have backed health care developments for some time now—some of the largest U.S. REITs focus on health care—Canadians have been slow to embrace the segment.

Health care is seen by some respondents as an ideal defensive play. Demand for health care services is continually growing, and rents are stable or rising. Not surprisingly, competition for attractive health care properties is increasing.

Yet as governments and health care practitioners strive to control costs and improve efficiencies, the nature of health care real estate is changing. The key trend is toward fewer—but larger—medical offices. Individual doctors' offices are increasingly a thing of the past: more and more doctors are sharing spaces and costs, and even collocating with labs, walk-in clinics, and other complementary health care services in the same building.

This consolidation or concentration is giving property owners the opportunity to provide additional services beyond traditional property management. Many health care professionals have little time or desire to handle the administrative side of their practices, so some property owners are stepping in and offering administrative, technology, and other services to fill that need.

Seniors' Housing and Assisted Living

An aging population is also driving demand for retirement homes and assisted living complexes. Despite the fact that some sizable Canadian REITs are focused on this market segment, the current seniors' housing market in Canada remains highly fragmented among a number of smaller players, and some see opportunities for consolidation. The low Canadian dollar is also piquing foreign investors' interest: Some U.S. companies are already looking for acquisition opportunities in Quebec. Outstanding deals remain in short supply, however, and cap rates remain low.

However, respondents anticipate that baby boomers will upend traditional thinking in this sector. Rather than gradually moving

Exhibit 5-13 Projections for Canadian Population, Age 55 and Over

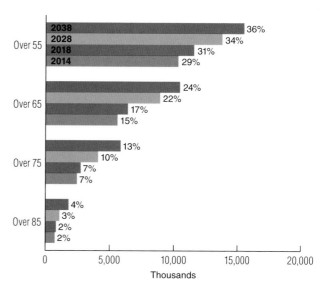

Source: Statistics Canada, Table 052-0005, Projected population, by medium projection scenario, as of July 1.

from a downsized home to an assisted living facility and then on to a full-care nursing home, some boomers may demand care continuity—and higher-quality care—in a single location. The problem is that much existing seniors' housing facilities cannot accommodate such demands, which could open up new opportunities.

Student Housing

Canada's growing student population needs affordable accommodation, and many universities are eager to offer guaranteed housing as a selling point to prospective first-year students.

The problem? Universities cannot afford to build the housing they so desperately want. In some cases, investors and developers are stepping in to meet the demand. Pension funds and institutional investors have entered into joint ventures to build new student housing properties. Elsewhere, developers have converted hotels into student residences, capitalizing on the similarities between the layouts of the two kinds of properties. Student housing remains very much a niche market, however, and one that is sensitive to demographic shifts. Some respondents are skeptical about its potential, citing the difficulty of achieving any sort of scale in the market.

Suburbs Resilient in the Face of the Urbanization Trend

There is just a "different mind-set" about the suburbs. "Tell me where the kids are going to go to school downtown—there are no high schools downtown." Not everyone is going to be able to come into the city until there are major changes. Families will continue to want to be in the suburbs.

The urbanization trend remains strong in Canada, but respondents dismiss suggestions that the suburbs are in decline. Every day, noted one commenter, people choose to exchange their small urban spaces for larger suburban living quarters.

Suburbs around Greater Toronto are also becoming more expensive due to government policies, immigration, and higher demand. Respondents believe that major investments in transit infrastructure, especially in and around Greater Toronto, will make the suburbs more attractive to a wider group of people. And as demand drives housing prices higher and higher in the core, they expect to see a growing number of people choose more affordable homes in the suburbs. Moving to the suburbs does not necessarily mean resigning oneself to a lengthy commute, either: many successful suburbs enable people to live, work, and play without having to travel all the way downtown, and the growing trend of working from home also reduces

Exhibit 5-14 Investment Recommendations for Commercial/Multifamily Subsectors in 2016

	Buy	Hold	Sell	2016 expected cap rate
Warehouse industrial	59.6%	21.3%	19.1%	5.9%
Medical office	54.3	31.9	13.8	6.4
Fulfillment center	52.4	42.9	4.8	6.0
Neighborhood/community shopping centers	42.2	36.1	21.7	6.1
Limited-service hotels	37.8	35.1	27.0	7.3
Apartment rental—affordable	35.0	40.0	25.0	5.6
Apartment rental—moderate income	35.0	38.8	26.3	5.3
Central city office	33.3	41.7	25.0	5.5
Student housing	32.4	47.3	20.3	6.0
Full-service hotels	27.0	48.6	24.3	6.8
Apartment rental—high income	26.3	32.5	41.3	4.7
Suburban office	25.0	41.7	33.3	6.6
R&D industrial	23.8	50.0	26.2	6.6
Regional malls	18.1	60.2	21.7	5.4
Power centers	13.1	44.0	42.9	6.4
Institutional rent for single family	10.3	47.1	42.6	6.0

Source: *Emerging Trends in Real Estate 2016* survey.

Note: Based on Canadian investors only.

commute times from the suburbs. Some people, in fact, may be choosing where they live first, based on affordability, and then choosing where they work, rather than the other way around.

In terms of commercial real estate, though, developers acknowledge that suburbs need more services, better tax incentives, and lower operating costs to compete with the downtown core.

Technology Creates New Opportunities and Challenges

"Data mining is a must-have. Continued investment in all aspects of technology needs to be a permanent line item in the budget."

E-commerce, cloud computing, mobile, and data analytics are just a few of the technologies that continue to reshape the way that people live and work each day. In the process, they are creating new opportunities—and challenges—for Canadian real estate players.

Respondents noted numerous ways that technology is changing how they do business. They're harnessing the power of data to make better business and marketing decisions and improve their financial reporting. They're using technology to improve how they design and build new developments and share knowledge across their enterprises. Some are using remote monitoring technology to deliver superior property management services to their tenants. And one respondent even noted that Google Maps allows potential investors, tenants, and buyers to view a building—and its surrounding neighborhood—well before making a visit in person.

Many respondents spoke of the way technology is changing the real estate needs of their retail tenants. Retail is evolving rapidly: e-commerce and a multichannel approach to engaging consumers become vital to retailers' success, and this is changing how they think about their physical space requirements. Many are rethinking the role of the store, and finding that smaller formats are all that is needed to serve consumers who are likely to view in person and buy online later. One respondent remarked that some retail tenants aren't looking for *stores* as much as *storerooms*—places to store their goods and package them for shipping to online purchasers.

The shift to a multichannel, e-commerce-driven retail model is about logistics more than anything, according to another respondent; as this changes how retailers move their products, it will also change how they look at real estate. Distribution facilities will become just as vital as physical shops—if they aren't

already. This will change how real estate players develop—or redevelop—their retail properties.

It's not just retail that is changing, either. Respondents are also coming to terms with how technology is changing the office real estate segment. Office workforces are flexible, nimble, and highly mobile; workflows and document management are increasingly digital and cloud-based. As a result of these shifts, office tenants are looking for smaller spaces—not in an effort to cut costs, but rather to adopt a more modern approach to what the office should be. Traditional offices—and even cubicles—are giving way to bench-style desks that support several workers and even more screens of various shapes and sizes. File rooms are disappearing; closets, drawers, and cupboards are being replaced by lockers.

Property owners are discovering that these changes in office space needs are driving up costs for office design, construction, and infrastructure. Renovating an office to suit a tenant is no longer just a matter of moving some walls around: as office densities rise and per-worker square footage drops, big investments in air conditioning, heating, washrooms, and other facilities are often needed. Some believe the real estate sector is underestimating the cost impact of these technology-driven changes.

As well, the increasingly critical role of technology in tenants' businesses is matched by their growing dependence on a stable supply of electricity. Outages are no longer a temporary inconvenience; they can bring a company's business to a complete and costly halt. Landlords report that their commercial tenants are demanding that they guarantee uninterrupted power, including immediate backup supplies in case of outages. Some tenants want these promises written into their leases.

Markets to Watch in 2016

"With the exception being Vancouver, the focus is shifting back to the east."

After three years of topping the Canadian markets-to-watch list, Calgary and Edmonton have slipped to mid-table as Vancouver, Toronto, and Montreal rise to the top.

Overall, respondents rank Vancouver as the top investment, development, and housing market in Canada this year. However, investor interest is definitely moving eastward as well, with four eastern markets in the top five. Several interviewees felt that the stable industrial outlook in both Toronto and Montreal

Exhibit 5-15 Markets to Watch: Overall Real Estate Prospects

	Investment	Development	Housing
1 Vancouver	3.62	3.27	3.96
2 Toronto	3.58	3.23	3.54
3 Montreal	3.17	2.99	3.36
4 Ottawa	2.94	2.82	3.33
5 Saskatoon	3.02	2.83	3.18
6 Winnipeg	2.95	2.75	3.20
7 Edmonton	2.66	2.58	3.65
8 Halifax	2.80	2.75	3.23
9 Calgary	2.98	2.67	2.86

1	2	3	4	5
Abysmal	Poor	Fair	Good	Excellent

Source: *Emerging Trends in Real Estate 2016* survey.

Note: Based on Canadian investors only.

positions those markets to benefit from U.S. economic growth and a lower Canadian dollar.

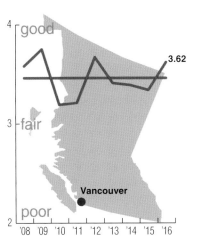

Vancouver

"Vancouver continues to be an in-demand marketplace to be for all real estate. There is a lot of available capital. The number of purchasers for large-dollar land deals has increased significantly from a few years ago, when there were maybe three bidders; now there are six or seven—quite a lot of foreign money as well."

Vancouver's economic growth may have hit a recent peak in 2014, but growth in 2015 and 2016 is still expected to remain strong, with gross domestic product (GDP) growth at 3.1 percent in 2015 and forecast GDP growth of 3.2 percent in 2016. Manufacturing, transportation, and warehousing are likely to

drive this growth in 2016, owing to the Canadian dollar's weakness against the U.S. dollar. The construction sector will be kept busy by a number of larger-scale mixed-use development projects in 2016; some observers believe that the industry could also benefit should the low Canadian dollar attract further additional foreign interest in Vancouver housing.

From a real estate perspective, "more of the same" seems to be Vancouver's mantra. Foreign investment still flows into Greater Vancouver's residential sector, though some foreign investors are now diversifying into the retail, office, and even agricultural sectors. The ongoing flow of international investment is still driving up prices, particularly for single-family homes; this has some Vancouver-area employers worried about their ability to attract and retain staff who are being priced out of the market. It is also giving rise to concerns that governments will come under pressure to bring foreign investment under some degree of control.

Rental developments are in the works in Vancouver; some estimate that some of these projects are aimed at the rental market. In retail, outlet and destination malls are proving popular, but traditional retail in Vancouver's downtown is seeing some softening. There also are some concerns about office vacancy rates, which at 10.4 percent in the second quarter of 2015 are Vancouver's highest in a decade. The high cost of living is making it harder to attract head offices and other major firms to the city, and it's not at all clear how long it will take for the market to absorb all the space that is available now—or becoming available in the next year.

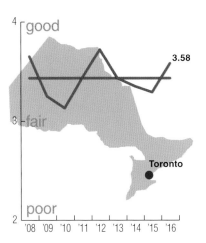

Toronto

Toronto achieved its strongest economic growth in four years in 2014 at 2.9 percent, and 2015 and 2016 are expected to be even better, with forecasted growth rates of 3.1 percent and 3.2 percent, respectively. While many industries are expected to play a part in this growth, key drivers include manufacturing, transportation, and warehousing, as well as trade and business services. Once more, the disparity between the U.S. and Canadian dollars, as well as low energy prices, are seen as playing a positive role in spurring economic activity. Several ongoing publicly funded construction projects—notably the city's ongoing waterfront redevelopment, Union Station's expansion, the Spadina subway extension, and the Eglinton Crosstown light-rail line—may offset any potential drop in residential building activity in 2016.

Overall, the Toronto market continues to have picked up where it left off last year—but investors and developers are acting with a bit more caution. Companies are still buying properties and investing in new developments, but they are being more selective and choosing opportunities that tick most, if not all, the boxes. Not surprisingly, infill developments and redevelopments remain high on the agenda, given Toronto's commitment to intensification. Prime examples of this include ongoing development in the city's South Core and West Don Lands districts. Mixed-use projects combining commercial, retail, and residential are increasingly attractive.

The outlook for Toronto's office market is fairly comfortable. Rents and cap rates are flat, causing investors to pay close attention to fundamentals in order to make money on projects. While 3.6 million square feet of new Class A space is under construction and slated to come on stream in the next couple of years, two-thirds of this space is preleased. Furthermore, vacancy rates, at 7.3 percent, are among the lowest in Canada. While there may be little worry over top-tier office properties, respondents worry that the Class B properties "left behind" may experience rent pressures.

The retail outlook also is *generally* positive. Urban retail is very strong: nearly every new project features some retail component to attract buyers and/or tenants. Destination retail such as outlet centers continues to perform well, and large regional shopping centers such as Yorkdale are very strong. Respondents also report that strip plazas that are anchored by grocery store or drugstore tenants also are doing well. However, power centers appear to be waning. Many tenants, it seems, had contingency leases that allowed them to break their lease or to negotiate lower rents if an anchor tenant left. Investors holding properties that were home to now-defunct Canadian retailers foresee a challenging time ahead.

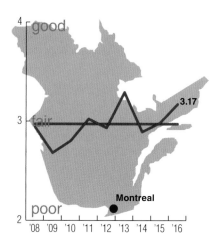

Montreal

Respondents feel that Montreal's economy is in for a period of stable but relatively low organic growth, though the region's GDP is projected to grow 2.6 percent in 2015 and 2.7 percent in 2016—the fastest rate of growth since 2002. Major infrastructure spending should benefit the construction sector, though whether this will offset any potential slowdown in housing starts remains to be seen. Once more, lower energy prices and a lower Canadian dollar are viewed as a boon for local manufacturers.

Montreal's suburban population continues to fall as baby boomers join generations X and Y in the urban core to embrace the live/work/play lifestyle. Condo development is set to take a breather, however, after the building boom of recent years. Retail remains an area of some concern in the core. The Rue Ste. Catherine redevelopment project has not yet resulted in an influx of luxury retailers. Outlet and strip malls on the outskirts of Greater Montreal are performing quite well, but the market can support only a small number of such destination retail developments. Office vacancies are very high—10.6 percent in second-quarter 2015—and some believe it could take five years to fill the space. Midtown Montreal is increasingly attractive to new businesses, especially those in the information, communication, technology, multimedia, and video game industry. Midtown offers businesses a location that is close to the downtown core, public transit, and other transportation—at more affordable rates.

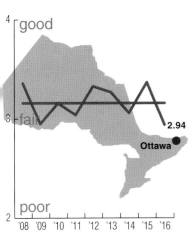

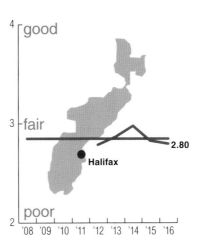

Ottawa

Public sector austerity measures have kept the government-dominated economy of Ottawa relatively stagnant in recent years. The outlook for 2015 and 2016 is a bit brighter, though: the federal government is expected to post a C$1.4 billion surplus in 2015–2016, and further public sector spending cuts are expected to be minimal. The region's goods production sector is projected to expand by 1.7 percent in 2015 and by 2.5 percent in 2016.

The business services sector also is set to grow significantly faster in 2015–2016 by 2.4 percent and 2.6 percent, respectively, buoyed by a strong technology sector and heightened investor interest in a number of Ottawa startups. Slow demand for single-family homes and a possible oversupply of multiresidential units are clouding the forecast for residential building, but the construction industry should be well supported by infrastructure projects in 2016.

Overall, however, Ottawa's aging infrastructure and the prospect of a change in Canada's federal government is dampening investors' attraction to the market, despite signs of an economic upturn and falling office and industrial vacancy rates. Ottawa's retail segment also looks poised to enter a transition period in the aftermath of major chain closures.

Halifax

Halifax's economic growth is expected to rebound strongly to 3.1 percent in 2015 from 1.7 percent in 2014, and maintain the pace in 2016 at 2.8 percent. A decline in primary industry and utilities output should be more than offset by growth in both manufacturing and construction. Increased shipbuilding and aerospace activity should provide a welcome boost to the manufacturing sector; the construction sector will benefit from several public sector projects and ongoing work on major mixed-use commercial developments.

The prevailing view is that Halifax's residential market will remain strong, and housing construction could pick up as a result of stronger economic growth. It's unlikely we'll see the sort of urbanization impact seen in other Canadian cities, as Halifax did not experience huge suburban growth in years past. Retail, which has struggled in the past couple of years, is attracting interest as regional development improves the employment picture. The office market, however, is a source of some concern: Businesses are rethinking space needs and searching for flexible, high-quality spaces that suit highly mobile, collaborative employees. Many current buildings simply are not equipped to accommodate those needs, and concern exists that businesses will flock to the newer properties coming on stream.

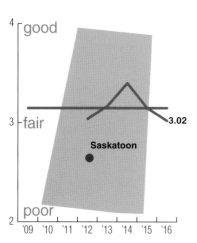

Saskatoon

Saskatoon's economic growth rate is expected to see a significant drop in 2015, bringing it to 1.8 percent from the 6.1 percent in 2014, a level just below the national average of 1.9 percent. The ripple effect of the slowdown in primary industry and utilities could cause slower growth across all sectors of the Saskatoon economy. Lower demand for housing is likely to slow residential construction, and commercial construction is likely to proceed cautiously as well. Real estate sales volumes are projected to shrink in 2016 from 6.1 percent to 3.3 percent, and this is expected to slow activity in finance, insurance, real estate, and other parts of the service sector. Yet while the energy sector's demands for manufactured goods are projected to be slow for the next couple of years, demand from the agriculture and timber sectors could in fact support manufacturing growth above the national average of 2.7 percent.

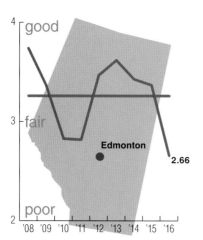

Edmonton

Edmonton's economy finds some stability due to public sector employment, but it will be hit hard by the drop in oil prices, tipping into recession in 2015 before showing signs of recovery in 2016—if oil prices stabilize and start to recover. Primary industry and utilities will contract significantly, and this will spill over into manufacturing, transportation and warehousing, construction, and trade. Manufacturers closely linked with oil extraction will struggle into 2016; others, however, could benefit from the lower Canadian dollar and lower transportation costs. High-profile projects in the city core may sustain the construction industry to an extent, but this may be offset by a slowdown in business investment and residential activity. While new condo towers rise up alongside the city's new arena, provincial museum, and other developments, the relative lack of retail and other amenities has some wondering whether these new towers will really have what it takes to lure people to move into Edmonton's downtown core. As well, respondents are very concerned about the outlook for Edmonton's office sector.

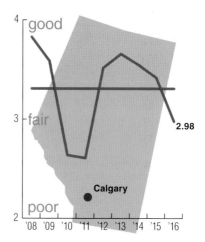

Calgary

Declining oil prices are expected to push Calgary's economy into recession in 2015 as well. While primary industry and utilities are taking the brunt of the downturn, manufacturing, construction, transportation and warehousing, wholesale, and retail also are projected to suffer. Residential construction is expected to drop over the next two years, as the economic slump slows net migration into the region. Nonresidential construction also is expected to slow, though several current projects should provide some buffer against the downturn. But while the downturn may have slowed down Calgary's real estate activity, it has not made real estate players especially pessimistic. Long experience with boom-and-bust cycles has helped Albertans excel at taking the long view: They are opting to hold onto what they have and wait as long as it takes before buying or selling.

Calgary has not embraced condo developments in the way Toronto or Vancouver has. Current buildings are selling, but no new condo projects are planned. In retail, companies are still digesting the impact of Target's exit; there is little appetite for new retail buildings, especially in the current environment, and so companies are instead focusing on redeveloping and rebuilding existing holdings. On the commercial side, Calgary's underdeveloped hotel segment is set to welcome two new developments. The office segment, however, is keenly watching to see the impact of 2 million square feet of space coming on stream soon. Concerns over vacancies are rising—as are worries over the amount of subleasing going on as firms try to cut costs in a tough economy.

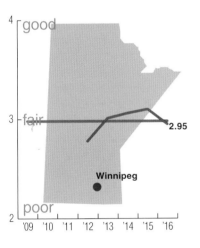

Winnipeg

Winnipeg's economy is expected to continue its steady growth at 2.1 percent in 2015 and 2.5 percent in 2016. The local manufacturing sector, which does not depend as heavily on the oil extraction industry, is benefiting from the lower Canadian dollar and reduced energy and transportation costs, and this should spark growth in U.S. exports. The retail and wholesale sectors should remain stable in the current economic environment, and business and personal services also are expected to do well.

Winnipeg's economic growth is persuading more people to stay put, it appears, as domestic out-migration to other provinces is falling. At the same time, Winnipeg is experiencing a rise in new migrants from across Manitoba and around the world. Despite this influx of people, construction activity may slow as housing starts fall into balance with population growth. A number of large nonresidential projects are slated to reach completion in 2015, which will further slow construction activity—though future infrastructure projects could pick up some of the slack.

Property Type Outlook

This year's survey responses reflect an outlook marked by cautious pragmatism. Some of the top-ranked property subsectors—for example, warehouses, fulfillment centers, and neighborhood or community shopping centers—are traditionally seen as defensive investments well suited to periods of slow economic growth.

It would be wrong to make too much of this and declare that Canada's real estate players are battening down the hatches.

Exhibit 5-16 **Survey Respondents' View of Their Local Markets**

	Average	Strength of local economy	Investor demand	Capital availability	Development/ redevelopment opportunities	Public/private investment	Local development community
Montreal	4.09	3.91	4.50	4.36	4.00	3.74	4.00
Halifax	3.96	3.87	4.43	4.21	3.86	3.67	3.75
Toronto	3.36	2.67	3.50	3.50	3.00	4.00	3.50
Winnipeg	3.36	3.18	3.41	3.47	3.32	3.36	3.39
Ottawa	3.29	3.23	2.95	3.47	3.35	3.42	3.29
Vancouver	3.16	3.18	3.10	3.30	3.10	3.13	3.13
Saskatoon	3.10	3.29	2.86	3.29	3.14	3.00	3.00
Edmonton	3.00	2.75	2.88	2.63	3.25	3.17	3.33
Calgary	2.83	2.62	2.62	3.00	2.92	2.80	3.00

Source: Emerging Trends in Real Estate 2016 survey.

Note: Based on Canadian investors only.

Exhibit 5-17 Prospects for Major Commercial Property Types, 2016 versus 2015 and 2014

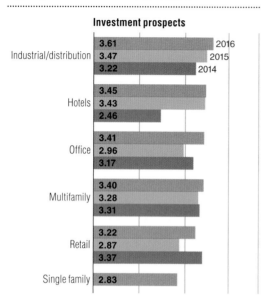

Investment prospects

	2016	2015	2014
Industrial/distribution	3.61	3.47	3.22
Hotels	3.45	3.43	2.46
Office	3.41	2.96	3.17
Multifamily	3.40	3.28	3.31
Retail	3.22	2.87	3.37
Single family	2.83		

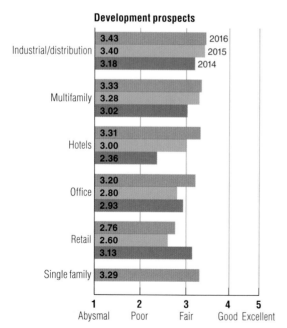

Development prospects

	2016	2015	2014
Industrial/distribution	3.43	3.40	3.18
Multifamily	3.33	3.28	3.02
Hotels	3.31	3.00	2.36
Office	3.20	2.80	2.93
Retail	2.76	2.60	3.13
Single family	3.29		

1 Abysmal 2 Poor 3 Fair 4 Good 5 Excellent

Source: *Emerging Trends in Real Estate* surveys.
Note: Based on Canadian investors only.

Warehouses and community shopping centers may be defensive plays, true—but they're also sectors well positioned to benefit from stable domestic consumer demand and the prospect of rising exports to the United States.

The results also point to other areas of optimism for the Canadian market. Investors are keen on the medical office sector, which is poised to benefit from favorable demographic trends and create opportunities for higher yields. Investors' interest in mid- and high-income housing rentals also is strong, and these sectors are set to capitalize on the rising numbers of Canadians choosing to rent rather than own.

Retail

"There is a trend for the consumer to spend more on quality of life than on hard assets—today it's more about the lifestyle than owning a BMW, people want balance in their life."

The rise of e-commerce and changing consumer behaviors are driving profound shifts in Canadian retailing, with significant implications for retail real estate. Retailers are rethinking their real estate needs in the online shopping era. Smaller store footprints, locations that combine both retail and distribution functions, and click-and-collect facilities will become increasingly common. Destination retail properties—outlet malls or large centers with premium brands—are poised to do well as Canadians search for memorable shopping experiences along with good deals. In Toronto, urban retail, especially as part of a mixed-use development, is seen to be strong, since collocating the two greatly appeals to target demographics. An influx of luxury brands is providing a welcome boost to the retail market in Vancouver, Montreal, and even Calgary to some extent.

Recent retailer exits from Canada and other recent chain closures are creating sizable challenges for some retail real estate investors. The loss of like anchor tenants is opening the door for shopping centers' smaller retail tenants to break their own leases—or lower their rents. Meanwhile, new anchor tenants are not easy to find, compelling some players to look at repositioning these larger spaces. Ultimately, investors in these anchorless shopping centers and suburban big-box retail spaces face limited growth prospects in the years ahead.

Purpose-Built Multiresidential Rentals

Faced with rising and increasingly unaffordable housing prices, Canadians across the country are instead choosing to rent. And it's not just those priced out of the market who are renting: downsizers and retirees also are driving demand for rentals as they opt to turn their equity into cash. Rental demand is likely to remain strong in locations such as Montreal, where a traditionally strong rental market already exists—as well as centers like Toronto, with its housing prices and solid population growth. It is likely that we will see more condominium developments convert to rentals in the face of market demand.

Exhibit 5-18 **Downtown Class A Office Space, Second Quarter 2015**

	Space under construction (sq ft)	Under construction, percentage preleased	Market vacancy rate
Toronto	3,602,655	67.4%	7.3%
Calgary	3,813,310	67.1%	9.8%
Vancouver	1,112,140	36.6%	10.4%
Montreal	1,358,780	43.8%	10.6%

Source: JLL, "Canada Office Market Overview Q2 2015."

Exhibit 5-19 **Average Home Size, by Country**

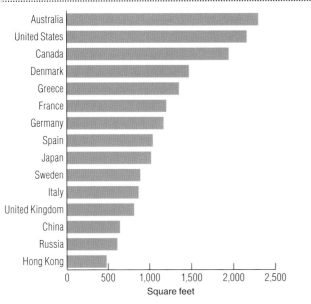

Sources: CommSec, Reserve Bank of Australia, United Nations, U.S. Census Bureau.

Some investors question whether returns on purpose-built multiresidential rental units justify the cost, and suggest that institutional investors and large REITs that have been focused on this segment are the players most likely to stay with rental property holdings over the long term.

Single-Family Homes

"We need to be able to create affordable housing in the city to be a socially responsible and competitive city."

Respondents are keenly aware of widespread concerns over the lack of affordable housing, especially single-family homes. They are frustrated by the popular opinion that they realize massive profit margins on residential developments and therefore must be able to absorb rising building costs, development charges, and other government-mandated costs. It is simply not true, they assert, and they make it clear that increases in development charges and other costs have a direct consequence on home prices and housing affordability. Developers believe that if the trend continues, Canadians will grow more comfortable with living in smaller spaces, like many of their peers around the world (see exhibit 5-19). Either that, or they will come to terms with commuting long distances in order to find affordable housing. There isn't much of an alternative. Some interviewees also suggested that a need exists for better communication among government, industry, and consumer groups—and better information about what is really happening in Canada's housing markets—in order to address the affordability issue.

Condominiums

"There is a real trend of people accepting smaller living spaces. The design of the space must be efficient and well thought out."

As single-family detached homes become increasingly unaffordable for many Canadians, respondents have noted that people are growing more comfortable with the idea of living in smaller spaces. Demand is good, with both younger Canadians and older retirees eager to purchase condos and embrace the urban-core lifestyle. Vancouver and Toronto are still seen as attractive, safe places for foreign investment capital, which is keeping condo demand steady. Condos continue to perform well in most other Canadian cities as well.

Industrial

"Logistics buildings are still in demand to support increases in online ordering together with smaller retailer footprints. In Ontario, this is encroaching on the 'greenbelt,' so players either need to redevelop older sites or go beyond the greenbelt."

Distribution and logistics are driving industrial activity, as e-commerce grows and consumers and businesses alike demand shorter and shorter delivery times. Height is in demand, with 30-foot ceilings far more attractive to tenants than the squat, sprawling properties suited to yesteryear's manufacturing sector. Redevelopment is popular now, since developers find that retrofitting older buildings to suit modern tenant needs is more cost-effective than new development.

Office

"Leasing and space layout strategies are not oriented on top management anymore. It used to be that the president or CEO made all the decisions on leases and real estate. Now companies must listen to, understand, and adapt to what employees want."

Canada's office segment will see millions of square feet in new office space come on stream over the next couple of years. Concerns over finding tenants for this new space vary across the country, and the numbers tell the tale. Vacancy rates are up across the country, rising slightly in Toronto (5.7 to 7.3 percent) and Montreal (9.4 to 10.6 percent) and spiking more sharply in Calgary (2.5 to 9.8 percent) and Vancouver (5.9 to 10.4 percent). And while preleasing rates have improved in Toronto—from 56 percent last year to 67.4 percent this year—they have dropped in Calgary (75 to 67.1 percent), Vancouver (60 to 36.6 percent), and Montreal (58 to 43.8 percent).

Industry players are particularly worried about the prospects for the older properties left behind. Of chief concern is that these older buildings are not well suited to the needs of the modern workplace. Where once presidents and CEOs made office space decisions, today it is just as likely to be the human resources team. Private offices are shrinking to make way for large, open collaborative spaces; bike racks and showers are needed more than parking spaces; sustainability, energy efficiency, and multipurpose or outdoor spaces are becoming "must-haves." Older offices, designed with yesteryear's workplace needs and attitudes in mind, must be upgraded to stand a hope of competing.

Expected Best Bets for 2016

Retail in mixed-use developments. Mixed-use projects combining condominiums, offices, and retail space are still going strong in most Canadian urban centers. And as people continue to move closer to the core (at least, those who can afford to), demand for retail and other amenities is rising. Retailers are eager to meet the demand with smaller, innovative store formats—which bodes well for developers with space to lease.

Destination retail remains a solid play. While the need for retail in the new core developments gets much of the attention, respondents also see strong opportunity in destination retail. Consumers eager for a bargain—or an outstanding shopping experience—have proved more than willing to make the trip to outlet malls and similar retail destinations.

Eastern Canada industrial property, especially distribution. The growth of e-commerce and shifting consumer behaviors is compelling companies to improve their supply chains and achieve ever-shorter delivery times. As a result, demand for industrial buildings and land that is suited for distribution centers is rising, particularly in eastern Canada. Suburban properties and industrial campus developments are attracting investor interest, since moving away from the urban center provides better transportation access.

Redevelopment of older properties. Respondents expect to see significant investment in the redevelopment of older buildings in the years to come. Companies are eager to upgrade their properties to keep pace with new developments coming on stream, to address tenant demands, and to capitalize on the trend toward multiuse building in the urban core.

In the west, bargain hunters are on the prowl. Investors will be keeping a keen eye on companies whose exposure to western Canadian real estate puts them at risk. We may see more consolidation among REITs, as well as more activity by investors keen to acquire valuable assets at a discount by targeting troubled REITs and other companies.

Condos and rental apartments are still a good bet. The market for condominiums remains solid in many parts of the country, particularly in Greater Vancouver and Greater Toronto, especially as single-family home prices continue to rise. Yet it's not all about condos any longer: as many Canadians opt to rent, demand for rental apartments also is growing.

Suburbs await an exodus from the core. As it gets harder and harder to find affordable housing in Canada's urban cores, frustrated homebuyers will start looking further afield. Investors and developers are keen to welcome them back to the suburbs.

Interviewees

Aegis Property Group
Jim Kinzig

Aegon USA Realty Advisors Inc.
Donald P. Guarino Jr.
Lyndsay Schumacher

AEW Capital Management
Michael J. Acton
Marc L. Davidson
Pamela J. Herbst
Jonathan Martin
Robert J. Plumb

Agellan Capital Partners
Frank Camenzuli

AIG Global Real Estate
Robert Gifford

Alston & Bird LLP
Jason W. Goode
Rosemarie A. Thurston

Alterra Group Limited
Robert Cooper

Amacon
Bob Cabral

American Realty Capital Hospitality Trust Inc.
Ed Hoganson

Amicus Investors
Steve Utley

Angelo, Gordon & Co.
Reid Liffmann
Mark Maduras
Adam Schwartz
Gordon Whiting

Apartment Investment and Management Company
Ernie Friedman

APG Asset Management US Inc.
Steven Hason

Apollo Global Management
Colburn J. Packard

The Armour Group Limited
Scott McCrea

Aspac Developments Ltd.
Gary Wong

Aspen Properties Ltd.
Greg Guatto
Scott Hutcheson

AvalonBay Communities Inc.
Kevin O'Shea

Avison Young
David Eyzenberg
Richard Hanson

AXA Real Estate
Olivier Thoral

Axiometrics
Ron Johnsey

Balboa Investments Inc.
Timothy Blair

Bank of America
Kenneth Cohen
Christopher Rogalski

Bank of America Merrill Lynch
Jeffrey D. Horowitz
Ron D. Sturzenegger

Barclays Capital
Ross Smotrich

Basis Investment Group LLC
Mark K. Bhasin

Bell Partners
Durant Bell

Bentall Kennedy (Canada) LP
Remco Daal
Paul Zemla

Berkshire Group
Chuck Leitner

BlackRock
Jack R. Chandler

Blackstone
Ken Caplan

Bluerock Real Estate LLC
James G. Babb III

BMO Harris Bank
Hans C. Geyer
Aaron Lanski
John Petrovski

Bosa Development Group
Nat Bosa

Boston Properties
Mike LaBelle
Owen D. Thomas

Brandywine Realty Trust
Tom Wirth

The Bristol Group
James Curtis

Brixmor Property Group
Michael Pappagallo

Broccolini Construction Inc.
Michael Broccolini
Paul Broccolini
Emilio Minotti

Bucksbaum Retail Properties
John Bucksbaum

Build Toronto Inc.
Bill Bryck

Buzz McCoy Associates Inc.
Bowen H. "Buzz" McCoy

Cadillac Fairview Corporation
Cathal O'Connor

Canadian Apartment Properties Real Estate Investment Trust
Tom Schwartz

Canadian Tire Real Estate Investment Trust
Ken Silver

Canderel Management Inc.
Daniel Peritz

Canyon Capital Realty Advisors
Jonathan P. Roth
Maria Stamolis

CapRidge Partners
Steve LeBlanc

Capright
Jules H. "Jay" Marling

Carey Watermark Investors Inc.
Michael Medzigian

Carmel Partners
Christopher Beda
Michael LaHorgue
Dennis Markus

CBRE
Richard Barkham
Tom Frye
Anthony Long
Jeanette Rice
Bob Sulentic
William C. Yowell III

CBRE Commercial Tri-State Region
Mary Ann Tighe

CBRE Econometric Advisors
Jeffery Havsy

Charles River Realty Investors
Brian Kavoogian

Charter Homes & Neighborhoods
Robert P. Bowman

The Chevy Chase Land Company
Thomas Regnell

Choice Properties REIT
John Morrison
Bart Munn

CIBC World Markets
Benjamin Tal

Citi Private Equity Services
Michael Dwyer

Clarion Partners
Doug Bowen
Stephen J. Furnary
Hugh McDonnell
Tim Wang

Cogir Management Corporation
Mathieu Duguay

Colliers International
George S. Iliff
Andrew Nelson

Columbia Property Trust
James Fleming
E. Nelson Mills

The Concord Group
Richard M. Gollis

Connecticut Retirement Plans and Trust Funds
Cherie Santos-Wuest

CoreLogic
Frank Nothaft

Cornerstone Real Estate Advisers LLC
Scott D. Brown
J.D. Sitton

Corporate Office Properties Trust
Bill Barroll
Steve Burdorick
John Norjen
Roger Waesche

CoStar
Hans Nordby

CRE Finance Council
Stephen M. Renna

Cresa Ottawa
Darren Fleming

Crow Holdings
Harlan Crow
Anne Raymond

Crown Realty Partners
Michael Pittana

Cubesmart
Chris Marr

CUNY Baruch
David Shulman

Cushman & Wakefield
James Carpenter

DDR Corp.
David Oakes
Luke Petherbridge

Desjardins Gestion internationale d'actifs inc.
Michel Bédard

DG Group
Robert De Gasperis

DiamondRock Hospitality Company
Mark Brugger

Digital Realty Trust
William Stein

DivcoWest
Mike Carp

Dividend Capital Group, University of Denver
Glenn Mueller

Donahue Schriber
Lawrence P. Casey
Patrick S. Donahue

Dorsay Development Corporation
Geoffrey Grayhurst

Douglas Elliman
Faith Hope Consolo

DRA Advisors LLC
Paul McEvoy

Dream Global REIT
Jane Gavan

Dream Unlimited Corp.
Michael Cooper
Jason Lester

D.R. Horton Inc.
David Auld
Jessica Hansen

Easterly Government Properties Inc.
William C. Trimble III

Education Realty Trust
Randy Churchey
Christine Richards

Eii Capital Management
Michael Hudgins

Empire Communities
Paul Golini Jr.
Andrew Guizzetti
Daniel Guizzetti

Empire State Realty Trust
David Karp

EPIC Realty Partners
Gord Thompson

Equus Capital Partners Ltd.
Arthur Pasquarella

Essex Property Trust Inc.
Mike Schall

Exeter Property Group
Ward Fitzgerald

FelCor Lodging Trust
Richard A. Smith

First American Title Insurance Company
David J. Feldman

First Niagara Bank
Christophe P. Terlizzi

First Potomac Realty Trust
Andrew P. Blocher

Fonds immobilier de solidarité FTQ
René Lamarche

Forest City Commercial Group
James Ratner

Forest City Enterprises Inc.
David LaRue
James Prohaska

Franklin Street
Andrew Wright

Fraser Valley Real Estate Board
Rob Philipp

The Furman Company
Stephen P. Navarro

GAW Capital Advisors (USA) LLC
Ashbey Chang
Roman Nemtsov

Getty Realty Corp.
Chris Constant
David Driscoll

GID
Robert DeWitt
Brian O'Herlihy
Bill Roberts

Ginkgo Residential
Philip Payne

Glenborough LLC
Alan Shapiro

Goff Capital
John Goff

Great Gulf Group
David Gerofsky

Great Point Investors
Joseph Versaggi

GreenOak Real Estate
Sonny Kalsi

Greenpark Group of Companies
Carlo Baldassarra

GreenPointe Homes
Margaret Jennesse

Greystar
Bob Faith
Bill Maddux

Grosvenor
Robert Hess

GTIS Partners
Amy Boyle
Steven Gorey

Guggenheim Partners
Kieran P. Quinn

Harrison Street Real Estate Capital
Thomas R. Errath

Harvard Management Company
Dan Cummings

Hawkeye Partners LP
Bret Wilkerson

HCP Inc.
Lauralee Martin

Health Care REIT
Scott Estes

Heitman
Mary Ludgin

Hersha Hospitality Trust
Ashish Parikh
Jay Shah

HFF
Riaz Cassum
David Keller

Hilton Worldwide
Kevin Jacobs

Hines
Thomas D. Owens

Holborn Group of Companies
Joo Kim Tiah

HomeFed
Paul Borden

Homestead Capital
Gabe Santos

Hopewell Residential Communications Inc.
Paul Taylor

Hospitality Properties Trust
John Murray

Hudson Realty Capital LLC
Arthur Brodsky
David J. Loo
Richard Ortiz

Hyde Street Holdings LLC
Patricia R. Healy

IDI Gazeley
Matthew Berger
Bryan Blasingame
Laura Taylor

Inland Private Capital Corporation
Rahul Sehgal

Institutional Real Estate Inc.
Geoffrey Dohrmann

International Council of Shopping Centers
Michael P. Kercheval
Jesse Tron

Intracorp Group
Kevin Smith

Intracorp Projects Ltd.
Kristen Devaney

Invesco
Scott Dennis

Irish Residential Properties REIT plc
David Ehrlich

Island Capital Group
Robert C. Lieber

iStar Financial
Jay Sugarman

Ivanhoe Cambridge
Jeff Brown
Sylvain Fortier
William R.C. Tresham

Jamestown LP
W. Jeffrey Beckham
Renee T. Bergeron
Matthew Bronfman

J.P. Morgan Asset Management
Nancy E. Brown
Wayne A. Comer
Kevin J. Faxon
Preston D. Meyer
Hilary J. Spann

JWI Investments
Scott J. Weiler

Kensington Realty Advisors
James Lee

KHP Capital Partners
Joe Long

Kimco Realty Corporation
Conor C. Flynn
David B. Henry

KingSett Capital Inc.
Jon Love

Klingbeil Capital Management
Kevin Kaz

KMK Capital Group of Companies
Justin Ladha

Lachman Associates
Leanne Lachman

Ladder Capital Finance LLC
Greta Guggenheim

Lakeview Homes Inc.
Anthony Montemarano
Rino Montemarano

Larson Realty Group
Eric Larson

LaSalle Investment Management
Jacques Gordon
Lynn Thurber

Linneman Associates and American Land Fund
Peter Linneman

Lionstone Investments
Doug Prickett

M3 Capital Partners
Dan Poehling

Macerich
Thomas E. O'Hern

Mack-Cali Realty Corp.
Michael DeMarco
Tony Krug

Madison Group
Miguel Singer

Makena Capital Management LLC
Susan Meaney

Manulife Financial
William Secnik
David Shaw
Joseph Shaw

Manulife Real Estate
Catherine Barbaro
Ted Willcocks

The Mathews Company
Bert Mathews

Mattamy Homes Limited
Brian Johnston

MedProperties Group
Jesse Ostrow

Merrill Lynch, Pierce, Fenner & Smith Incorporated
Ken Cohen

MetLife Real Estate Investors
Mark Wilsmann

Metzler North America
Donald Wise

Mid-America Apartment Communities
Eric Bolton

Moody's Investor Service
Merrie Frankel

Morgan Stanley
Peter C. Harned
John Klopp
Candice Todd

The Muldavin Company
Scott Muldavin

Murray Hill Properties
David Green
Norman Sturner

Newland Communities
Vicki R. Mullins

New York Life Investments Management LLC
Christian McEldowney

New York Life Real Estate Investors
Brian Furlong
Steve Repertinger

Ninety Degree Enterprises
Guy F. Jacquier

Noble Investment Group
Jim Conley

NORC at the University of Chicago
Jon Southard

Northwest Healthcare Properties REIT
Paul Dalla Lana

NPV Advisors
David Walden
John Wrzesinski

Odebrecht USA
Eric Swanson

Ohana Real Estate Investors
Sarah Mancuso

Orlando Corporation
Bill O'Rourke

Otéra Capital
Alfonso Graceffa
Edmondo Marandola

Pace Properties
Robert Sherwood

Pacific Urban Residential
Arthur Cole
Alfred Pace

Paladin Partners
James Worms

Parkway Properties
Jason Bates

Pension Real Estate Association
Greg MacKinnon

Penwood Real Estate Investment Management LLC
John Hurley
Karen Nista

Phillips Management Group
Kevin G. Phillips

Piedmont Office Realty Trust
Donald A. Miller

Playa Hotels & Resorts BV
Larry Harvey
Bruce Wardinski

Plaza Retail REIT
Kevin Salsberg

PM Realty Group
John Dailey

PNC Real Estate
Diana Reid

PNC Real Estate Finance
William G. Lashbrook

Polaris Development
Ziyad Mneimneh

Principal Enterprise Capital
Emily Slovitt

Principal Real Estate Investors
Jodi M. Airhart
Marty Cropp
John Frandson
Michael Lara
Jay Skelton

Prologis
Hamid Moghadam

Prudential Real Estate Investors
Kevin R. Smith

PSP Investments
Neil Cunningham

Quantum Properties
Diane Delves

RBC Capital Markets
Carolyn Blair
Dan Giaquinto
Gary Morassutti

RCLCO
Gregg Logan

Real Estate Capital Partners
Paul Doocy
Michael Fruchtman
Sylvia Gross

RealNet Canada Inc.
George Carras

Real Property Association of Canada
Michael Brooks

Realty Income
Paul Meurer

Reardon Realty
Gary Reardon

Regency Centers
Martin E. "Hap" Stein

Regent Homes
David McGowan

REIS Inc.
Ryan Severino

RioCan REIT
Rags Davloor
Edward Sonshine

RLJ Lodging Trust
Ross Bierkan

Rockpoint Group LLC
Keith B. Gelb
Thomas Gilbane

Rockwood Capital
Robert Gray

Rosen Consulting
Kenneth Rosen

RXR Realty
Frank Patafio

Sabra Healthcare REIT Inc.
Richard K. Matros
Talya Nevo-Hacohen

Sentinel Real Estate Corporation
David Weiner

Seven Hills Properties
Luis A. Belmonte

Shelter Rock Capital Advisors
Walter Stackler

Shorenstein Properties LLC
Glenn Shannon

Silverpeak Real Estate Partners
Arash Dilmanian

Silverstein Properties
Marty Berger

Skanska USA Commercial Development Inc.
Catherine Pfeiffenberger

Sonnenblick-Eichner Company
David Sonnenblick

Stag Industrial
Ben Butcher

Starwood Capital Group
Marcos Alvarado
Jerry Silvey

State of Michigan Retirement Systems
Brian Liikala

State Teachers Retirement System of Ohio
Stanton West

Steadfast Companies
Ella Neyland

Stockbridge
Jack Melkonian

Summit Industrial Income REIT
Ross Drake
Paul Dykeman

Taubman Centers
Robert Taubman

TCF National Bank
Richard Baer

TCN International
H. Ross Ford

Terreno Realty Corporation
Michael Coke

Thibault, Messier, Savard et Associés Inc.
Martin Galarneau

TIAA-CREF
Gerald Casimir
Richard Coppola
Thomas Garbutt
Robert Villamagna

TIAA Henderson Real Estate
James Martha

Tideline Partners
Lev Gershman

Timbercreek
Ugo Bizzarri

TMG Partners
Michael Covarrubias

Toronto Port Lands Company
Michael Kraljevic

The Townsend Group
Jennifer Young

TPG Real Estate
Jamie Sholem

Trepp LLC
Matt Anderson
Thomas Fink

Trinity Development Group Inc.
Michael Dobrijevic
Fred Waks

Turner Impact Capital LLC
K. Robert Turner

UBS Global Asset Management (Americas) Inc.
Lee S. Saltzman

UBS Realty Investors LLC
Gary Gowdy
Matthew Lynch

Unaffiliated
Connie Moore

United Properties
John Breitinger

Value Acquisition Fund
Andrew F. Cates

Velocis
W. Fredrick Hamm
Michael S. Lewis

Ventas
Debra Cafaro
Bob Probst

Vornado Realty Trust
Steve Theriot

Wachtell, Lipton, Rosen & Katz
Adam O. Emmerich
Robin Panovka

WAFRA
Frank Lively

Watson Land Company
Bruce A. Choate

Williams Preferred Apartment Communities
John Williams

W.P. Carey
Trevor P. Bond
Hisham Kader
Katy Rice
Thomas E. Zacharias

Wright Runstad & Company
Greg Johnson

Sponsoring Organizations

PwC real estate practice assists real estate investment advisers, real estate investment trusts, public and private real estate investors, corporations, and real estate management funds in developing real estate strategies; evaluating acquisitions and dispositions; and appraising and valuing real estate. Its global network of dedicated real estate professionals enables it to assemble for its clients the most qualified and appropriate team of specialists in the areas of capital markets, systems analysis and implementation, research, accounting, and tax.

Global Real Estate Leadership Team

R. Byron Carlock Jr.
U.S. Real Estate Leader
Dallas, Texas, U.S.A.

Mitchell M. Roschelle
U.S. Real Estate Valuation and Due Diligence Services Leader
New York, New York, U.S.A.

Frank Magliocco
Canadian Real Estate Leader
Toronto, Ontario, Canada

Kees Hage
Global Real Estate Leader
Luxembourg, Luxembourg

Uwe Stoschek
Global Real Estate Tax Leader
European, Middle East & Africa Real Estate Leader
Berlin, Germany

Craig Hughes
U.K. and Global SWF Real Estate Leader
London, U.K.

K.K. So
Asia Pacific Real Estate Tax Leader
Hong Kong, China

www.pwc.com

The mission of the Urban Land Institute is to provide leadership in the responsible use of land and in creating and sustaining thriving communities worldwide. ULI is committed to

■ Bringing together leaders from across the fields of real estate and land use policy to exchange best practices and serve community needs;

■ Fostering collaboration within and beyond ULI's membership through mentoring, dialogue, and problem solving;

■ Exploring issues of urbanization, conservation, regeneration, land use, capital formation, and sustainable development;

■ Advancing land use policies and design practices that respect the uniqueness of both the built and natural environments;

■ Sharing knowledge through education, applied research, publishing, and electronic media; and

■ Sustaining a diverse global network of local practice and advisory efforts that address current and future challenges.

Established in 1936, the Institute today has more than 35,000 members worldwide, representing the entire spectrum of the land use and development disciplines. Professionals represented include developers, builders, property owners, investors, architects, public officials, planners, real estate brokers, appraisers, attorneys, engineers, financiers, academics, students, and librarians.

ULI relies heavily on the experience of its members. It is through member involvement and information resources that ULI has been able to set standards of excellence in development practice. The Institute has long been recognized as one of the world's most respected and widely quoted sources of objective information on urban planning, growth, and development.

Patrick L. Phillips
Global Chief Executive Officer, Urban Land Institute

Kathleen B. Carey
Chief Content Officer

ULI Center for Capital Markets and Real Estate
Anita Kramer
Senior Vice President
www.uli.org/capitalmarketscenter

Urban Land Institute
1025 Thomas Jefferson Street, NW
Suite 500 West
Washington, DC 20007
202-624-7000
www.uli.org